AGENTS OF CHANGE @ WORK

Attitude and Approach

Bill Walsh

First Edition

NOTAE Publishing, Lisle, Illinois

Agents Of Change @ Work

For further information please contact:
William J. Walsh
1496 Culpepper Dr.
Naperville, Il., 60540
(630)- 369-1905

Published By NOTAE Publishing, Lisle IL.
Printed in the United States by Beta Graphics Corporation, Aurora Il., 60506-7900

ISBN 0-9701621-5-4

Single copies of this book may be obtained by sending a check or money order in the amount of US $19.95 to:

NOTAE Publishing
PO Box 1183
Lisle IL, 60532

Price includes shipping and handling.

Quantity discounts are available to organizations purchasing ten or more copies. Fax (630) –416-8770 to request specific information.

Visit our website www.notae.com
"The Business of Change"

TABLE OF CONTENTS

Acknowledgments

This book would not have been possible without the careful guidance and encouragement of the following individuals:

Paul Douglas
Doug Forker
Jared Finney
Tom Glennon
Terry Sidlow
Jack Walsh

Each spent many hours reviewing and reshaping the ideas presented on these pages based on their outstanding experiences in the automotive, appliance, aerospace, pharmaceutical, and medical fields. All have seen great change in their respective industries, and each understands firsthand what it takes to "make it happen" in today's ever changing world of enterprise.

I would also like to thank David Firszt, my wife Pat, my son Bob, and the staff of Beta Graphics Corporation for their many valuable suggestions in the development of a final manuscript.

B.W.

Preface

This is a book about the skills and the work ethic needed to be a job-effective worker as the 21st century unfolds. It is a time of dynamic and often chaotic change, driven by intense global competition, an economy increasingly dominated by services, and the ever-widening "digital divide" of the workforce, which has been brought about by the computer and the Internet. In this never-before world of accelerating change, there are only the "changers," who make it happen, and the seemingly helpless bystanders—the "changees."

At the enterprise level, one need only to look at the latest additions and deletions of companies who make up the Dow Jones Average or Fortune 500 rankings to be reminded of this blunt truth. At the level of the individual, today's successful worker must be highly adaptable to change.

Much is written today about the need for leaders in industry. This book is intended to give concrete expression to this somewhat elusive concept of "leaders" by portraying them as *agents of change*. It is hoped that these pages will be of value to all those intent on becoming an enterprise leader. In other words, those who would like to go a big step beyond being a "good" employee.

But it should also be helpful to two other large groups of workers. First, there are those who are just starting their careers. Although superbly trained academically and eager to succeed, they seek practical guidance on the day to day approach to job-effectiveness. The second group are those already employed, perhaps for a long time. Many have been uncomfortable observers of a shift in their own attitudes towards their jobs. A polar shift from a self-fulfilling sense of "I can't wait to get there in the morning" to an energy sapping feeling of "I can't wait to get home at night." These people have been aptly called the "painfully employed." Frequently, this seasoned group of workers vaguely blames this mind shift "on all the changes." Or, perhaps they specify the problem to be their boss one week, foreign competition the next, and the new office computer system a month later. No matter what, most desperately want to recapture that earlier desire of becoming an outstanding contributor. But somehow it all *seems to be* beyond their control.

One cannot be part of an organization for any length of time without observing that there are people, at every level, who are consistently job-effective in their efforts. They succeed in their work efforts no matter who the boss happens to be, where the competition is coming from, or which office software suite happens to be in vogue.

Characteristically, these individuals bring to their work a certain "can do" attitude and a certain systematic approach to their tasks. An attitude and an approach that re-enforce each other in such a way as to transform these special individuals from being a member of that large group of hard working, albeit struggling employees, to that select cadre who "make it happen."

Most of my career was with Eaton Corporation —thirty-four years to be exact. Eaton is a global and diversified manufacturer of highly engineered products, that serve the vehicle, construction, commercial, aerospace, and industrial markets. The company has annual sales approaching $9 billion dollars, and more than 60,000 employees located at 195 sites in 22 countries. For nearly ninety years Eaton has been highly regarded by its customers for the quality of its products and services, and the commitment of its employees to high business ethics.

The breadth of Eaton coupled with the length of my tenure provided me with many different work experiences. I worked excitedly during my early years with R&D teams in the initial development of automotive airbags, cruise control systems and truck skid controls. I also slugged it out for many years in a penny–pinching operations environment, that made automotive and appliance controls—a favorite target of cost and quality competition from overseas. As a director of engineering, I have had the opportunity to work with large numbers of people at every level of the organization, from senior executives to the latest June crop of trainees. I participated many times on varied team assignments with Eaton associates in Europe, Mexico, Brazil, and Australia. No matter what business they were in, what their job responsibilities were, or in which country they were located, there were invariably people I met, who clearly were different from all the rest. These "make-it-happen" people were the company's *Agents of Change*.

This book is intended as a road map on the journey to becoming an agent of change. Hopefully, it will convince you that the trip is well worthwhile. But simply reading it will not get you to this rewarding destination anymore than reading a travel map will magically transport you from one place to another. You have to be willing to make the journey yourself!

The "Discussion Problems" included at the end of each chapter are intended to get you started on that road. Carefully thought-out answers that you develop, individually or by sharing experiences in a group seminar will provide you with many raw ideas that can be refined into a working plan. Then the real part of the journey begins; it is a journey of practice, practice, and practice. Fortunately, that journey becomes ever easier as you proceed down that road.

One final thought on the personal side: writing a "how to" book on becoming a job-effective agent of change is uncomfortable in the sense that it is much like writing a tome on personal holiness. Each paragraph has caused me to confront and relive anew my own past job performance sins. A useless wish is that I had spent as much time thinking about job-effectiveness in the early years of my career as I did towards the end. On the other hand, if my observations of the many outstanding agents of change I met over the last forty years prove accurate and helpful to others, I will have been granted the next best thing.

Bill Walsh.

Chapter 1-The Changed World of Enterprise.

You see things; and you say, "Why?"
But I dream of things that never were; and
I say, "Why not?"

- "Back to Methusalah,"
- George Bernard Shaw,
- 1921

Agents of Change

This book is for all of those who are of the mind to ask "why not." And these pages are an exploration of those personal attributes and skill sets that will characterize the "why-not" job leaders of this new and dynamic century. The job-effective workers, the sought-after, rewarded, and self-fulfilled employees of the 21st century will be *Agents of Change.*

Change is inevitable. But to be a helpless bystander to change is not; rather that is one choice. Change agents make the other choice. They are the self-motivated people who sense opportunities coming from every direction, and who have the desire to make positive change happen, everyday, in their places of employment.

Of course, change agents are nothing new to us. They are the heroes and heroines of history. Lincoln, FDR, and Martin Luther King were change agents. So too, were Mother Theresa and Albert Einstein. Each asked "why not," and found an answer that challenged and changed how we as a people think.

Outstanding agents of change are to be found in every worthwhile human endeavor, and the ever-expanding universe of enterprise is no exception. Thomas Edison and Henry Ford are legendary entrepreneurial change agents as is Bill Gates. Each had a dream—a light in every room, an automobile in every garage, or a computer on every desktop. So, they each changed the way we live.

Change agents need not be legends. Look around any fast growing enterprise, and surely you will observe agents of change hard at work. No matter what their mission, they share one thing in common. They have clear answers, or more precisely, a strategy about[1]

1) *Who* are their customers?
2) *What it is* that their customers need now?
3) *How to* change things in order to meet that need?

It has been said that the essence of strategy lies in an organization's ability to create tomorrow's competitive advantages faster than its competitors can mimic the ones it possesses today. This statement is nothing less than a prescription for perpetual change. It is also the credo of today's change agents.

Change Agents are loyal team players, but they are also an organization's "movers and shakers." They lead as well as they follow, and they enjoy doing both. More tellingly, true change agents are the masters of the difficult discipline of self-adaptation—the ability to change themselves.

An agent of change is easy to spot. He or she brings to their work both a "can-do" attitude and a systematic approach. Together they are interweaved like the woof and warp threads of a strong fabric. The positive attitude underscores the approach, and the approach to job tasks continually re-enforces the attitude.

Finally, we might point out what a change agent is *not*. He or she is not a maverick. Mavericks are self-appointed, solo performers who seek change strictly on their own terms, and outside the bounds of the organization. A maverick delights in disruption, and rarely effects lasting change. The true change agent on the other hand is an empowered individual, an organizational catalyst, who systematically accomplishes meaningful change by working within the organization.

Each of us instinctively would like to be an agent of change in our work endeavors. As much as any schoolboy wants to catch the tie-breaking pass, we want to make a real difference in our own world of enterprise. But just as in football, a lot of exciting "offense" in business is dependent upon having worked-out, beforehand, some very solid "defense." So, understanding the blocking and tackling aspects of being an agent of change also has to be an equal concern.

In developing our understanding of a *job-effective* change agent we will sequentially examine:

1) The greatly increased need for agents of change in the rapidly evolving world of enterprise.
2) What it means to work "job-effectively."
3) A systematic approach for accomplishing *customer-valued* change.
4) The attitudes—what we will call the working ethic—of a job-effective change agent.
5) The change agent's role in the team environment.
6) The roles personal core competencies, strategic intent, and knowledge management play in our overall job-effectiveness.
7) The seven levers by which we can effect meaningful enterprise change.

The Growing Need For Change Agents In The Workplace.

Real change involves real risk. Therefore, "been there, done that" has long carried a lot of weight in the business world. Until relatively recently, any needed change in an enterprise followed a kind of food chain paradigm. That is to say that the small, everyday tactical changes were morsels to be bitten off at the lower levels of the organization. The major strategic changes—the really big fish—on the other hand, were untouched fare to be passed-up to the highest levels. The guiding presumption being, of course, that the organization's hierarchy had the most experience, or, at the very least, a "higher helicopter" view of the shifting needs of the enterprise.

Under this paradigm, the senior leadership, after first developing an awareness of their organization's changing strategic needs, would carefully deliberate their options. They would then periodically choose and reset their organization on a new, and hopefully more rewarding course.

Their mandated plans were effectively carried-out in practice by a grid of intermediate managers that in the very large corporations might be a dozen levels deep. This managerial grid was, by design, interlocked through defined accountabilities, and bound together by a common purpose.

A carefully planned, top-down business strategy, borne of long experience, and executed by a cohesive managerial network can provide the established enterprise with insuperable advantages. This is especially true in a situation where the customers are predictable, the competition well defined, and the underlying changes in relevant technology gradual. In other words, when the business parameters of tomorrow are really not much different than that of today, give or take a few percent. Unfortunately, as we will see over and over again in the following pages, this kind of slowly and smoothly changing world of enterprise no longer exists. It is now a world of large and unpredictable discontinuities.

Some New Problems With The Old Ways.

Starting in the 1980's, large and parallel changes in the overall business environment clearly began to overload the long established, but often ponderous, chain-of-command operating structures of many corporations. Three changes, cosmic in nature, were particularly challenging. These were:

1. The emergence of a truly global economy.
2. The ever-increasing economic importance of services as opposed to the production of goods.
3. The game changing impact of new technologies, especially in the information arena.

Global Competition: An Unending Battle.

In 1982 world trade in terms of exports from all countries amounted to 1.8 trillion dollars. Just fifteen years later, this export trade had more than tripled to 5.5 trillion dollars. The long predicted "globalization" of the economy had truly arrived! Significantly, the US share of this export trade stayed all but constant over this same fifteen year period–just nudging up from 12.2% to 12.4%[2]. The world trade pie had become much larger, but at the same time there were many more and hungrier nations intent on sharing in it.

None of us really need astronomical trillion dollar trade statistics to know that we live in an increasingly globally economy. A Sony TV now sits in our den where an RCA long stood; a new Toyota berths along side the old Ford in the garage; our shirts were made in Sri Lanka; and our "dress-up" shoes come from Italy. Our latest, have-to-have acquisition—a miniature cell phone—was designed and made in Finland.

We also do not need to search to the right of the decimal point to know how difficult it is to change our year to year standing in the very competitive arena of world trade. We better than know it: we *feel* it. We feel it each morning as we drive out of the sub-division and wonder whether or not our neighbor, Al, has found a job after "being-out" for the last seven months. And we see it as we pass the boarded-up eyesore of an electronics plant that was the town's great hope just five years earlier, or the smokeless ruins of a steel mill that stood for nearly a century.

We have reluctantly come to understand that this peaceful, yet unending, and often painfully competitive war is the engine of our global economy, and in many ways our human progress. As such, it is also the harbinger of unending opportunities for the change agents of enterprise. Opportunities to create new products and services, or at least to re-make old ones quicker, better, and cheaper.

At Your Service Madam.

The odds are seven to ten today that you are classified by the government as a "service worker." Obviously, the term covers a rather broad expanse; the barely sixteen year old behind the counter at your nearby Mc Donald's is considered to be a service worker, but so too, are the steely-haired neurosurgeons at John Hopkins University Hospital. Those involved in providing hotel lodging or information processing, are in the service industry, as are those engaged in advertising, education, or repairing automobiles and TV's. Because of this generalization, service workers are most easily defined by what they are *not*. A person who does not work in manufacturing, agriculture, or mining is with some few exceptions a service worker.

What is so significant about service work—a mega change in the world of enterprise—is the dramatic rate of increase in the number of these workers since 1970. Service workers in the US have more than doubled to 98 million in that time frame. This figure now accounts for 75% of the workforce. Contrast this with manufacturing employment that has remained virtually constant at 20 million, and agriculture and mining, both of which have even declined a bit to around five million.[3]

Especially high employment growth areas have been financial and health services. In even small towns we are now likely to see banks on all four street corners, each a veritable supermarket to meet every conceivable financial need. The same is true in health care; the solo family doctor and county hospital have given way to clinical teams of "x-ologists" working in highly specialized facilities from birthing centers to hospices.

This same high service growth phenomenon has taken place in both retail and wholesale trade. The downtown, one-stop department stores of yesteryear have now given way to mile after mile of low-flung strip malls, each an Americanized market bazaar of highly focused goods. In the communication and transportation sectors, restaurant and entertainment services, personal care and repair industries, the overriding service themes are the same: abundance, complicated choices, and diversity.

New services continue to multiply faster than rabbits! For example, how many new phone companies and new rate plans come out each year? Or would it be easier to count them monthly? There seems to be little evidence that this rapid proliferation of services will level off anytime soon.

By their very nature, services require a high degree of informed, on-the-spot, and adaptive decision making on the part of both the providers and customer. Unlike a high-volume, assembly-line product, successes in services tend to be won one sale and one customer at a time. As we will see in the following chapters, this creates in every enterprise enormous needs and opportunities for "knowledge workers" to function as job-effective agents of change.

The Game Changing Impact Of New Technologies.

The third major change in the business environment that we have noted is the impact of new technology. The breadth and depth of our modern technology landscape is so vast it is hard to bring it into focus. Technological change agents surprise us daily with new developments in microprocessors, wireless communications, nano-mechanics, genetic engineering, molecularly designed drugs, and space exploration.

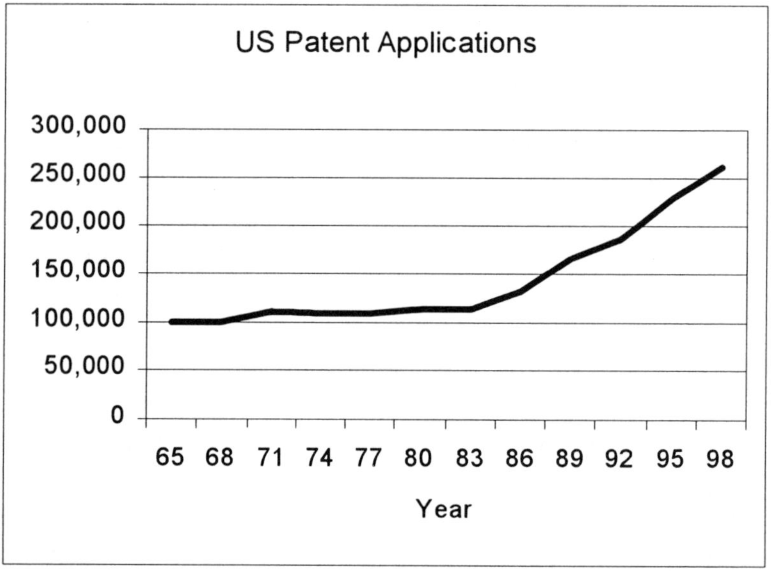

Figure 1.1. US Patent Applications Begin To Accelerate Around 1985.

New technology also plays a major role in enabling old products and services to be freshly delivered in more expansive and efficient ways. This is the story of the "dot-com" start-ups and e-commerce. So, we need to find a measuring stick that can capture the astounding rate at which technology is moving. Figure 1.1 is just such a yardstick. It plots the number of patent applications submitted to the US Patent Office over the last thirty-five years[4]. Admittedly, it is only a surrogate measure; not every advance in technology is patentable; and the perceived value of patents changes with enforceability trends. Nevertheless, the figure shows the dramatic growth in patent applications starting around 1985. Prior to this time the yearly rate of patent applications hovered around 100,000, but after 1985 we see an upward swing to a level that triples to 300,000 as the century ends, again with no sign of a leveling-off in site.

Clearly the exploding growth of enterprise is in no small part rooted in the growing abilities of technological change agents to master the art of innovation.

The Wall Street Outlook.

Government statistics about such things as exports, employment trends, and patent applications provide us with a lot of solid information. Unfortunately, it is information about what has already happened a year or more ago. In other words it is a history lesson. As change agents we really want to know about what is going to happen in the future. This desire leads us to figure 1.2. It plots the change in the Standard and Poors index of 500 stocks over the last twenty years. The S&P index is a useful and broad, relative measure of what investors are willing to pay for a market basket of stocks.

Now, the key point is that investors buy stocks in anticipation of future sales growth and profits. So, at very least, the S&P 500 index gives us an indication of what people believe about the future of enterprise. It is a kind of fortune telling in the most literal sense.

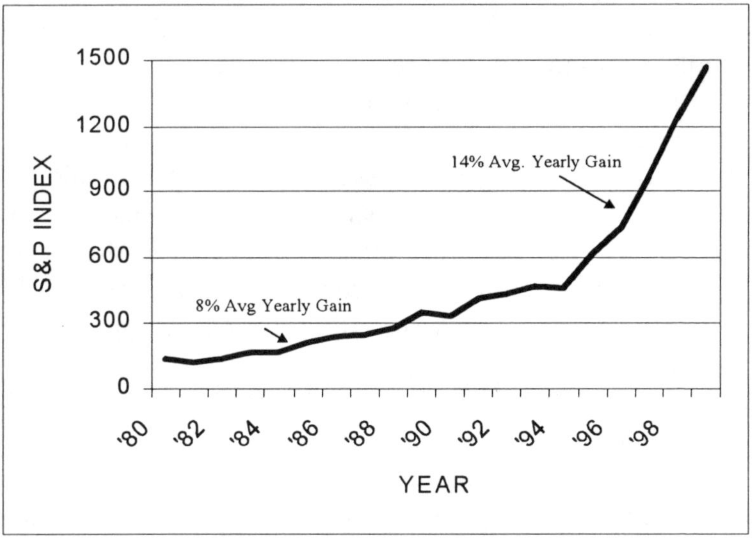

Figure 1.2. Investors Show Greatly Increased Confidence In The Long Term Growth and Profits of Enterprise[5]

Throughout most of the 1980's and into the early 1990's these investors bid up S&P index prices about 8 % per year. Along about 1994, however, the relative cost to buy this market basket of stocks abruptly began to increase to about 14% annually.

Clearly, investors at this point developed a sustained belief that the opportunities for the future growth and profits of enterprise would be significantly greater than in the past. Increased sales and profits that would arise from the confluence of growing productivity, innovative technologies and services, and global market expansion opportunities. All of which are summed up in the phrase "the new economy."[6]

Needs Fathered By Chaos.

We have seen how globalization, the growing dominance of services, and new technology are causing dramatic economic change. Interspersed with these three mega-trends have been other needs for "make-it-happen" workers brought about by shifting inflation/deflation scenarios, de-regulation of key industries, the fall of communism, a deepened concern for environmental pollution, and the militant rise of consumerism.

This turbulent confluence of change has often been described as "chaotic." In any event, it has overwhelmed the long-established ways of managing change. The littered business landscape of the last twenty years provides unmistakable evidence. The grim tale is constantly retold by downsizings that are followed by shotgun mergers, and wholesale outsourcings signaled by managerial delayerings. There seems to be no indication that the heavy price of change is slackening. For example, in 1999, despite a full-employment economy, announced white-collar layoffs reached 700,000, a figure that exceeds every other year of the decade.

New Roles For Everybody.

Executive responsibility for the management of change is greater than ever. Indeed, it might be argued that this attention to change is now more nearly the total rather than a piece of an executive's jobs responsibilities. But it in itself is a rapidly changing responsibility: Rather than attempt to puzzle-out the impact of each new change-challenge for themselves, the senior leadership must now continually search out and empower, through *remote trust,* the best informed change handlers within their organizations. And if necessary, search outside the enterprise. The old executive approach of "Tell me, this morning, *all* that I need to know about the Internet," no longer works! Simply because the Internet, already vast and complex, will surely not be the same next quarter and quite possibly next week.

The only valid answer to the many profound changes rapidly taking place across the broad frontiers of business is an equally rapid and in depth response across entire organizations. All the members of an enterprise, managerial and non-managerial alike must be prepared to assume proportionate and coordinated roles as active agents of positive change. Roles where on-the-scene flexibility and spontaneity complement executive experience and deliberation. And where real-time information continually tempers long range planning.

Thus, there is a growing need for agents of change to populate the sales force and the design room, work the plant floor, and man the accounting and quality control offices. For, the successful enterprise of the twenty-first century is no longer primarily a ranked army of executives, managers, professionals and laborers. Rather it is an organizational continuum of change agents harmoniously working together.

A Possible Solution Offered By Mother Nature.

In Biology there is a concept known as "adaptive radiation." It suggests to us how organizations can adapt to today's challenges. This theory holds that under the influence of changes in the external environment some species take on, over time, *enhanced* physical characteristics that enable them to better adapt to the new living conditions.[7] For example, through evolution some members of a bird species might develop a longer beak. This longer beak allows them to ferret out a group of abundant insects, which tend to burrow more deeply in the ground. These variant birds, being better fed, and hence better suited to survive than their short-beaked cousins, become dominant over time. Technically, they are said to have "radiated."

In some instances, the changes in physical characteristics of these adaptively radiated species are so profound that they begin to resemble an already existing species. When this further step occurs it is known as "evolutionary convergence."

Adaptive radiation and evolutionary convergence are precisely what are taking place in many high growth corporations today! Adaptive radiation is being driven by the increasing importance of the knowledge worker, the information processing power of the ubiquitous computer, and the global grasp of the Internet. Evolutionary convergence, on the other hand, is demanded by the need for spontaneity and flexibility inherent in a competitively racing, service-dominated, and technology driven world.

Together these two related trends are combining to effect rapid and meaningful organizational change by extending the decision making power to all working levels of an enterprise. Within much broader limits than former times, non-managerial workers need to share in the planning, controlling, and organizing of their own efforts, if a business is to be successful.

Similarly, the traditional manager must be prepared to adaptively radiate into a more viable species. It is the species of the *leader*. The leader provides his working team more with tomorrow's vision than today's direction, and more with a compass setting than a detailed road map. The managerial leader empowers as much as he controls, and he learns from his team as much as he teaches.

Together, there is evolutionary convergence talking place on both sides of the managerial and worker ranks. This species convergence point is today's Agent of Change!

Summary.

In this introductory chapter we developed some basic notions of just what it means to be an agent of change—a make-it-happen worker. We have also taken a "higher helicopter" look at the new economy. Over the last twenty years we have seen near-universal and chaotic enterprise challenges brought about by:

1. Rapid globalization
2. The increasing dominance of a service oriented economy.
3. The explosion of new technologies, especially in the information arena.

These three synergistic trends continually demand responsive change at all levels of an enterprise. And hence, a need for empowered agents of change throughout an organization.

Discussion Problems.

1. Identify three people in your organization whom you consider to be "change agents." What common characteristics in attitude and approach to their work do they share?
2. Give several examples of recent assignments where you had the opportunity to function as an agent of change.
3. How have globalization, growth in services, and new technology impacted your organization over the last three years? What other outside forces have caused significant change in the way business is conducted?
4. In what ways do you see your job scope "adaptively radiating"?

Chapter 2- Zeroing In On Job-Effectiveness

In the introductory chapter it was stated that a job-effective agent of change brings to his or her work a certain *approach* and a certain *attitude*. In this chapter and in the next we will concentrate on approach. Our first order of business will be to develop a more objective sense of job-effectiveness.

A Look in Your Toolbox.

Think of your toolbox. Better still imagine you have just dumped the entire contents of the box out on the table. What would you find as you began to sort the tools into several piles? Probably you would first come across some of those basic tools you first acquired many years ago. Even today, you use them on virtually every job. Next, you might come across a few very special tools that you remember allowed you to do a super job on a complicated piece of work. Just seeing them gives a deep sense of accomplishment and pride.

You are likely to have a third pile of tools that you rarely seem to use. Perhaps, because you don't fully know how. They just sort of sit in the box; some are even beginning to rust. Lastly, there is a fourth pile that is starting to build-up on the table. In this pile are some really broken or blunted tools that just don't work very well, but for one reason or another you still find yourself reaching for them, especially when you are in a pinch.

This toolbox is not the one you keep in your basement or garage. It is much more useful and important than that. Rather, it is the one you bring to work everyday and carry home every night. This tool kit is what goes to make up your overall job-effectiveness.

Like our workshop toolbox, our job-effectiveness tool kit includes some very basic items, for example, our listening and analytical skills that we need for almost everything we are expected to do at work. They are like a hammer and screwdriver. Then, there are those special tools we are most proud of; the ones our peers consider us expert at using. Perhaps, it is the ability to close a difficult deal if you are a salesman, or the ability to figure out a complicated heat transfer problem if you are an engineer. Chances are we also have a few unused and even rusty tools in that box. Maybe it's that tough Statistics course we had way back in college, and have not used since.

If we are a little bit honest with ourselves as we search through our job-effectiveness kit, we realize that we are missing a couple tools that would allow us to do our jobs a whole lot better. Perhaps, we don't have all the skills we need to do coaching or counseling.

If we can be very honest with ourselves during this search, we probably will have to admit that we are also carrying a few things around in our box that we like to use as tools. But in fact, they hamper us from getting the job done smoothly. In a personal sense they are our blunt screwdrivers, slipping wrenches, and dulled saws. Through mindless inclination we just grab them into our hands whenever a tough situation comes up, and flail away. Being overly defensive in a meeting, or impatient with our sub-ordinates, are everyday examples. These kinds of tools have nothing to do with being a job-effective employee. Unfortunately, they are in the box cluttering things up, until we see them for what they are, and make the decision to toss them out. Cleaning-out and re-stocking our tool kit is one of the most valuable steps we can take in our job-effectiveness journey.

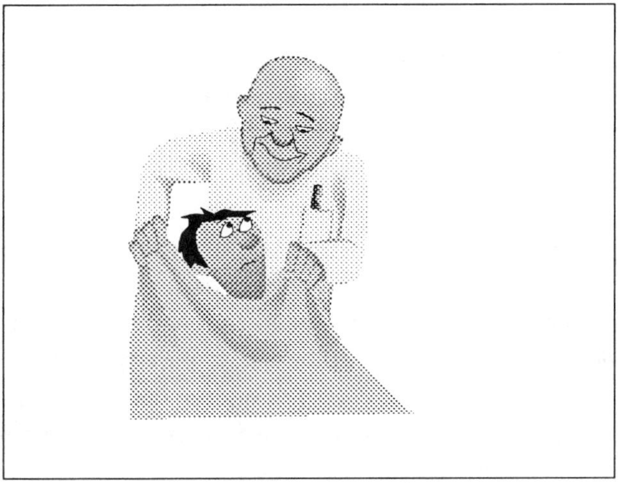

Defining Job-effectiveness.

Anyone, who has ever suffered through the three-week aftermath of a bad haircut, painfully understands the real meaning of job-effectiveness. We also understand, perhaps less well, that from time to time everyone of us gives some of our customers a "bad hair-cut" in its infinitely variable forms. There are product designs that don't always work; water-faucets that leak after we fix them; medical advice that is confusing; or long, staff reports that recommend nothing.

As we proceed in our study of the "right stuff" of a change agent, we will continually refine our notions of what we mean by job-effectiveness. To get started let us think of it as a threefold combination of our personal work ethics, the processes, and the acquired vocational skills that we use everyday to accomplish our work.

So, initially we can write a simple little equation:

Job-effectiveness = Personal Work Ethics + Work Process + Acquired Vocational Skills.

By our work ethics we really mean the personal qualities we bring to bear in getting a job done. Such attributes as the effort we put into a piece of work, our reputation among co-workers as to credibility, and our inclination to take the initiative, are all examples of job work ethics. The *work process* characterizes the systematic approach we typically use to achieve the desired result in an efficient manner. In other words, a good work process keeps us from getting the cart before the horse. Lastly, acquired skills represent our specialized knowledge or training in a particular discipline. They give each worker a certain degree of proficiency at performing specific job functions. Some of these vocational skills may be widely shared, such as the ability to manipulate spread sheets, or do word processing on the computer. Other valuable skills may be possessed by relatively few individuals. These relatively unique skills will be referred to as our *core personal competencies.* Cumulatively, these unique competencies contribute to the overall effectiveness of the organization by their very diversity in breadth and depth.

Job-effectiveness Is A Lot Like Golf.

In the game of golf many of us have learned the hard way that, sooner or later, we can improve our scores significantly by just taking a few lessons. By so doing, we more quickly learn that there are some inviolable rules of play; that there is a correct way to consistently swing a club; and that depending on where the ball happens to lie, some clubs are a lot more useful than others.

The same is true with our quest for job-effectiveness. There are certain rules that apply to all of us in the working environment. There is a correct and consistent process for performing work that adds up to high performance, and there are some tools in our bags that are a lot more useful than others in particular work situations. Also, like the game of golf, after we have taken a few lessons, real progress in job-effectiveness is going to depend on lots of real world practice.

Job-effective Work Pays Big Personal Dividends.

On a personal level, the job-effective individual has three real advantages in the workplace:

1. They are more likely to experience their job, most of the time, as a rewarding, self-energizing, and fun experience.
2. They are far more likely to keep their present position in bad times, and advance to a more desirable one in good times.
3. They are more likely to get the new job they want, and in a shorter time. Their past job-effectiveness will quickly surface in an employment interview in a way that even the most carefully crafted resume leaves flat on the paper.

The first point cannot be overemphasized. It is very rare to meet a lousy golfer who loves the game, or a good golfer who hates it. The same is true of our work. If we are consistently effective in our jobs, the overwhelming odds are that we will enjoy the "game." If not we may see ourselves, with some justification, as being unarmed, stalked, and hunted in an unending trek through the "industrial jungle."

So, although our final objective is job-effectiveness, our companion goal is job-satisfaction, hopefully, even to the point of job-excitement. Job-satisfaction is something we not only experience at work, but on the way home, during our leisure hours, and even as we sleep soundly at night. So Job-satisfaction is a very worthy prize.

Finally, while the emphasis of this book is on how to be a successful and effective employee, this point of view should not be mistaken for signing up for a lifetime vow of humble servitude. Indeed, quite the opposite! Good executives and good managers overwhelmingly are chosen from the ranks of good employees. And with their elevated responsibilities they continue to be good employees. That is to say they are just as adept at getting results *through their own personal efforts as* they are at leading the efforts of others.

Learning Job-effectiveness Is Not Like It Was In The Good Old Days!

Thirty or forty years ago, people who started their careers in large companies learned the basics of job-effectiveness, mostly, through daily doses of careful supervisory guidance by more senior employees. It was known as "OJT"or on-the-job-training. Companies of that time were highly structured from top to bottom with as many as eight to fifteen layers of officers, directors, managers, supervisors, and foremen. Each layer was able to focus on guiding rarely more than a handful of people directly under them.

Advice from the boss was always in abundance, whether one needed it or not. There was a humorous and much duplicated wall sign of that era, which neatly summed-up this whole approach. It read:

RULES FOR COMPANY DECISION MAKING

RULE #1: THE BOSS IS ALWAYS RIGHT!

RULE #2: IF THE BOSS IS WRONG CONSULT RULE #1

Paternalism was the operational style; organizations were as likely to refer to themselves as a "family" as a corporation. Moreover, the nature of most businesses, the products they provided to the marketplace, and the organizational structures, which managed them, seemed to change slowly, if at all. Competition in the marketplace was mostly within our own national borders, and in hindsight now seems to have been downright gentlemanly.

Individual responsibility and progression up the organizational ladder also tended to be rather slow and highly graduated. An engineer, for example, might spend a decade progressing through narrowly defined ranks as a Junior Engineer, Assistant Engineer, Associate Development Engineer, and Development Engineer before finally becoming a Senior Development Engineer. It was not until achieving this last position that the engineer could really feel that he or she had significant, independent design engineering responsibility.

Although this slow pace and resultant bureaucracy was often frustrating, it did have its redeeming features. First, unlike today, many employees could reasonably expect to spend thirty or forty years with a single company, and then be rewarded with a fairly generous, company-funded pension. Secondly, it really took some headstrong effort to screw-up along the way!

Scene 2000.

But now, let's fast-forward another thirty-five years. The dawn of the twenty-first century presents a radically different business scenario. Market competition has become global and unrelenting. Customer expectations of what constitutes quality products and services have increased dramatically, while the market life cycles of these products have contracted just as dramatically. Most significantly "time–to-market" response has replaced stability as the organizational hallmark.

Today, employees can expect to average seven or more job changes in their careers; their employers exit one long-held business in the same quarter that they acquire yet another unfamiliar one; and corporations narrow their product portfolios at the same time that they go global in their market outreach.

Organizationally, corporations, large and small, have de-layered management levels to less than half that of former times while spans of control have quadrupled. The role of the manager is now that of the charging and exploring visionary *leader.* Today's leader has little time left to be the watchful guardian of those beneath them. Besides, what was learned a decade ago in terms of technology, market dynamics, and organizational structures now seems largely irrelevant.

Employees are now referred to as "empowered associates." New employees, whether they are entry level or mid career, are expected to hit the ground running, and make a right-now contribution. On the job training for recent grads now means an assignment in Latin America or China, or perhaps three months rotation in each of three totally unrelated departments.

That old wall sign, "the boss is always right," has been replaced by a new one that proclaims:

> LEAD!....
>
> FOLLOW! .. OR..
>
> GET OUT OF THE WAY!

This threefold choice confronts every 21st century employee, everyday, who wishes to be an Agent of Change.

Fundamental to continually making the correct choice is the need for a strong and systematic approach to self-guided job-effectiveness.

Our Customers: Lighthouse Beacons of Job-Effectiveness.

One of the things that will help us in our search for increased job-effectiveness is to have a clearer idea of what it means "to work." So this is going to be our first order of business. Now all of us have some pretty definite notions of *why* we work:

1. We have a family to support.
2. We have car payments to make.
3. The bible says that man must atone for Adam's sin by the sweat of our brows.
4. We find our work professionally challenging.
5. We get to meet some interesting people.
6. Or perhaps, some combination of all of the above.

We also have a fairly precise idea of *what we do* at work; we teach children with learning disabilities; we run the shipping department; or we are a dermatologist. Lastly, most of us also have developed a pretty good way of keeping score as to *how we are doing* at our work by looking through that rear view mirror called "success." So, we constantly track how much money we made this year; how long since our last promotion; how many people now report to us; and how many people might have passed us along the way.

In a real sense, many of us can claim that we have a great deal of personal experience with working. But it is just that, *experience* that is seen through one set of eyes, and our very own personal point of view. Now, if all it took to be successful at anything was just lots of personal experience there would not be people losing and gaining fifty pounds six times over, or failing to par a single hole in a dozen rounds of golf. That is why there are thriving businesses for weight loss centers, golf pros, and all the rest of the people we call on from time to time to help us when we end up ship-wrecked on the rocky shoals of life.

Similarly, in our personal pursuit of job-effectiveness there are also many times when we are likely to find ourselves navigating through some dangerously murky waters, and it is not always easy for the "do-it-yourselfer" to keep from running aground. We need a lighthouse beacon!

Fortunately, in our working world, there is one bright beacon of helpful guidance that is always shining, day or night. It comes to us everyday from our *customers.* We recognize that these customers, to whom we sell our products and services, have a genuine interest in how well we perform. Our work output impacts them directly. Putting it in the simplest terms, they are counting on us. And since the customers are the one's that pay our salaries, at least indirectly, we have a matching genuine interest in wanting to do a good job. So we often remind ourselves that the customer comes first, the customer is king, or is always right.

All Of Us Have Lots of Customers.

While reflecting on this customer relationship we also need to broaden our concept of just who is a customer. As part of our quest to become more job-effective employees, we are going to define a customer as *anyone who is a downstream recipient of our individual work output*. So, in the course of a workday all of us will come in contact with lots of different customers. They are organizationally above us, below us, and beside us, even if we personally do not often deal with the so-called end or outside customers. For example, a secretary, who is given a set of notes from her boss to transcribe into a meeting report, should be regarded as a customer of that manager. In this case and many others there is an often-overlooked, mutuality to the customer-provider relationship.

Customers Help Us Set High Job Performance Standards.

One of the most important reasons for adopting this much-extended view of the traditional customer is that it helps us to consistently, and almost automatically, set the high job performance standards that underlie job-effectiveness.

In this connection, it is interesting to note that nobody praises an airline pilot, who makes safe landings *most* of the time, or a fire department that has a record of responding to ninety percent of all alarms in their district.

Yet in many organizational and commercial settings you usually don't have to look very far to find glowing performance ratings built upon such lukewarm comments as "Dave is on time for work most of the time ....," or excited company "PA" announcements that proudly shout, "LAST MONTH WE ACHIEVED 90% ON TIME DELIVERIES!!" ALL EMPLOYEES ARE INVITED FOR PIZZA....."

Of course, it is not difficult to explain the difference in attitude; with airlines and fire departments lives are at stake. And their customers, whether they are passengers or citizens, simply cannot accept any performance standard less than one hundred percent. Fortunately, for most of us employees in the business world, failure to perform our jobs to the highest standards does not jeopardize life. But just because we do not routinely deal with life threatening situations, it does not follow that there are no costly consequences for sloppy work efforts. Take the everyday case of the boss' meeting notes that need to be transcribed. If they are scribbled illegibly, it will certainly take the office assistant much longer to decode the notes, and get the report typed. So, there is a job efficiency loss. Of course, it may take the boss five more minutes to write the original notes neatly. But this might be only a fraction of the time that will be spent in work interruptions that follow, as he and the assistant attempt to clarify the notes he meant to capture in the first place.

Far worse is the situation if there is no correcting session, and a misstatement is broadly disseminated and acted upon. The simple dropping of a "no" or "not" in a sentence may result in a course of action being implemented that is a hundred and eighty degrees from that which the manager intended. And with far reaching consequences! Production inventory may not get ordered in time; a key sales contact may not be made; or a critical design change may not get implemented. Eventually, the mistake will probably be caught, and get straightened-out, but at a lost opportunity cost measured in time and dollars.

Organizations that operate in a perpetual panic mode—and there are many that do—invariably have developed a high tolerance, and seemingly, even an appetite for just this kind of "small" mistake. They find themselves creating costly and permanent mistake-covering structures such as inventory banks, assembly line checkers, and customer service reps that spend most of their working day apologizing.

Always keeping in mind the potential downstream impact of even small mistakes is one of the best self-checks each of us has in improving our overall job-effectiveness. Seeing every task that we do as one done for a customer gives us the proper focus. It is a focus we will build into our own tailored definition of job-effective work, which is our next step.

What Does It Really Mean "To Work"?

Besides viewing our work efforts in terms of their downstream customer impacts, we want to understand job-effective "work" in a way that transcends our own individualized experiences. We want to go beyond the *why,* the *what,* and the *how well* of our own personal situations and look at the very essence of productive work.

To do this we are going to have to develop a generalized definition of job-effective work that can be applied to an aerospace engineer, just as well as the assembly line worker; and, to the corporate CEO, just as validly as the young man starting in the basement mailroom. Granted these latter two may be separated from each other by thirty floors, and thirty years of hard work. And certainly the scope of their responsibilities will be different; being the architect of a major corporate restructuring is infinitely more complex than making sure that all affected departments get the re-organization announcements by 10:00 AM sharp! But under the definition of work that will now be proposed both the chairman and the mailboy will have been seen to accomplish the same thing.

We are going to define *job-effective* work to mean:

Job-effective Work = Creation of Change of Benefit to a Customer.

Line Up the Customer First!

Notice that an essential part of this job-effective work definition is to make sure that the change being created is of benefit to a customer. It bears a little closer examination. The sad truth of the matter is that not all work has a value to a downstream customer. The work product itself maybe original, well intentioned, and accomplished with only great effort and ingenuity on the part of the implementers. But if there is not a downstream customer willing to accept and able to benefit from the accomplished change, it has to be accounted a failure. Making sure you have a customer, who will benefit from, and desires the intended work, can sometimes be as tough and time-consuming as doing the actual work itself. Staff people know this only too well!

The larger the organization the more susceptible it is to this specific problem. Where the customer-benefit focus is not operative in a routine way because of organizational size, structural partitioning, or just plain poor communications, there is the ever-present opportunity for massive waste of work efforts. In any big organization there are all manner of unread staff reports, never used equipment, or mountains of data generated by an ambitious IT department that are closeted monuments to this point. The inscription on these monuments always reads the same, "We thought it would help your department!"

Let's Be Customer Focused, Not Customer-Driven.

As much as we must be sure that we have a downstream customer waiting to receive our work, it is essential that we have a proper working relationship with that customer. Earlier it was pointed out that we have an almost golden rule in the business world that the customer is always right. On the surface this is certainly a desirable attitude, but we have to be careful that we don't go too far overboard in this regard if we are going to do truly job-effective work. In particular, lots of organizations like to proclaim in their mission statements that they are "customer-driven" Naturally, these words sound very appealing to a potential client. But a blind subscribing to this mentality can lead to an unhealthy reactive type of relationship that actually impedes the job-effective work process.

After all, none of us would be inclined to put on our desks a framed sign that said we were "boss-driven," even if it happened to be true. It is not that we do not want to please our supervisor, or that we do not highly value our jobs. It is just not a healthy, mature relationship! For example, it would not be a job-effective physician who allowed her patients to cajole her into prescribing harmful medications, or other unwise treatments simply because that is what the patient demanded, or even sincerely believed was for the best.

In the everyday work world a similar kind of situation can arise. Reactive work efforts that are driven *solely* by the customer tend to be poorly defined, undertaken in haste, and open-ended. This invariably leads to unsatisfactory results, and rework. Instead, for maximum job-effectiveness, we want to have a mutually proactive relationship with our clients. Words more along the lines of being *customer-focused* or *customer-concerned* seem to describe this more desirable relationship much better. This proactive customer focus is the point of view we will adopt in our pursuit of increased job-effectiveness.

Seeing Ourselves As Agents of Change.

By always thinking of our work efforts in terms of implementing customer-desired change, we cease to see ourselves as just another pair of hands, however skilled. Instead, we become vital *Agents of Change*. Seeing oneself as a change agent gives a worker that proactive perspective that is so necessary to deal in today's world, where each new day is in some way very different than the one just ended. Agents of change imbue themselves with this new sense of empowerment that all organizations desire in their employees. An empowerment that so few feel secure in accepting. These empowered individuals become the "movers and shakers" that make the lasting differences in any organization.

Summary.

In this chapter we have focused on the meaning of job-effectiveness, and a definition of work that transcends our own individual experience. To these ends four key ideas have been proposed:

1. Our overall *job-effectiveness* is like a personal tool kit. It is made up of a habitual process and two sets of interpersonal and technical skills that we use everyday to accomplish our work.
2. A *customer* is considered to be anyone who is a downstream recipient of our work output. A constant customer focus steers us along the path of increased job-effectiveness. It also helps us to evaluate our own work products beyond our own immediate self-interests.
3. Job-effective work means that we consistently create change that is of benefit to a customer.
4. We want to serve our customers in a proactive manner and view ourselves as empowered agents of change.

Discussion Problems

1. What are the three best tools you have in your own personal job-effectiveness toolkit? Which tools in your kit might best be thrown-out?
2. What new job-effective tools would you like to acquire in the next year?
3. How many customers do you have in a typical day for your work output?
4. Give one example where a small mistake or oversight in your organization had a big impact? What percentage of people in your organization would you estimate are dedicated to correcting mistakes?
5. What do you believe are the mutual loyalty obligations between employers and employees?

Chapter 3- The Mechanics Of Job-Effective Work.

A Look At The Three Steps of the Work Process.

In the preceding chapter we defined job-effective work as the creation of change that is of benefit to a customer. We saw two advantages to this definition: first, it put us in the proactive role of being a change agent in a world that is thriving on change; second, it provided us with a vital customer focus.

There is a third advantage to this definition, which we now want to explore. The whole notion of "creating change" lends itself to being viewed as a process. And processes allow us to break down a given task into a series of simple, sequential steps that culminate in a result. In particular, we can analyze just what actions have to be performed, and what inter-personal skill sets are needed to successfully complete each step in a job-effective manner.

With a little thought, we can see that there are three steps that underlie the work process of creating beneficial change. These are:

1. Gather up all those factors that may have an impact on the desired change.
2. Figure out the best alternative(s) to make the change.
3. Make the change happen!

We now want to take a look at these three steps in some detail. For those of us who have already had a fair amount of experience in the working world, taking a close look at this process may seem a bit pedantic and uncomfortable. Uncomfortable in the same sense as taking a first lesson in golf, after having played the game a number of years. To have someone tell you, all at once, how to grip a club in a way that feels odd, keep your elbow straight, your head down, and your eye on the ball etc., can seem downright aggravating. Especially, after we have developed our own unconscious ways of doing it. After the first hour of the lesson we want to shout, "Just let me hit the darn ball my way!"

In our job efforts, just as in golf, most of us find ourselves, on occasion, missing the ball completely by making the wrong part, or hitting a wild slice by giving a presentation that completely veers-off the desired point. There are to be sure some "born athletes" in the working world just as there are in the sports domain. They do not need to analyze their working swing; they just seem to do everything right from the very first day they hire in. But for the majority of us, these next few pages might prove worthwhile.

A Baseball Player And A Doctor At Work.

To get familiar with the three-step change process outlined above, and its wide applicability, let us take a look at two very different kinds of work—that of a professional baseball player, and that of a doctor. First, we will analyze the case of the baseball player. Assume he is up at bat and waiting for the next pitch, and that the desired beneficial change is, at very least, to get on first base. As the batter waits for the ball to be thrown towards the plate he will likely take into account:

1. The mix of pitches the pitcher usually throws; fast balls, curves, inside or outside, etc.

2. The stance of the pitcher as he gets ready to deliver the ball.
3. The relative positioning of the other players in the infield and outfield.
4. The batters own recent success in hitting against this pitcher.
5. The last minute instructions of his coach as he left the dugout.
6. The pitcher's wind-up and release.

In taking into account these factors, and possibly others, the batter has just gone through the first step of the change process, which we call the *gathering* phase. The intent of the player at this point is to get as much useful information as possible before he moves into the second phase of the beneficial change process.

In the second step, all these inputs are assessed and a decision is made how best to implement the desired change. As the pitcher releases the ball the player will have to:

1. Decide that the ball will miss the strike zone and wait for a later pitch.
2. Bunt or fake a bunt.
3. Hit away.

This second, decision-making step is called the *evaluation* phase. At the end of this stage the player's mind has to be made up as to exactly what he intends to do!

With phase two completed, which in this particular instance lasts little more than a second, we come to the final element of the three-step process, the *action* or implementation phase. The course of action that the batter has elected to take must now be implemented, as the ball nears home plate. Let us suppose his decision is to go for a full swing and try for a home run. At this point the batter's entire concentration and energies are focused on the path of the oncoming ball, his swing timing, and control.

It is important to note that in each phase, the batter must call on some very different, but highly developed skill sets or competencies. In the gathering step the batter must be able to quickly "read" a whole set of input signals. The evaluation step calls for a split-second decision that can only come from lots of past experience in assessing these multiple and sometimes contradictory signals. Finally, in the implementation phase of executing his swing—what the pros call "muscle memory"— comes into play.

As a second example of a beneficial change process let us consider a doctor treating her patient. Again, the doctor tries to get as much "input" data as possible. This will likely include taking a personal history, physically examining the patient, and perhaps, ordering some laboratory tests. When all the information from the gathering phase is in her hands, the doctor makes a diagnosis, or in our parlance, an evaluation. Based on lab results, the complex of symptoms, and the patient's complaints, the doctor will prescribe a specific course of treatment from a number of available alternatives. Once, that has been agreed to by the patient, the action phase of the treatment begins, which in this case might be a prescription, surgery, or bed rest.

Take The Time To Do It Right Instead Of Over!

It is important to keep in mind what our objective is in each of the three steps of the work process. In the gathering phase we are interested in assembling as many pertinent facts as possible that help point the direction we need to go to effect the beneficial change. Facts are the foundation stones of the beneficial change process.

In the evaluation phase our objective is to converge on one or two alternatives that will best secure the desired beneficial change. Leading up to this judgment is a sorting out of the relevant information from the available pool of facts, the resolution of seemingly contradictory input, and lastly the pinpoint identification of still needed, yet missing data. In the many worlds of enterprise, sorting out what *actually is* from what *appears to be* can be quite difficult. A sound evaluation of a complex set of facts takes experience. This is where the judgment skills of employees with substantial background in a particular area are often a decisive advantage. Experience, properly balanced with real-time information, can be one of the most valuable tools in our job-effectiveness kit.

Credible evaluations also require time. That is why even a good hitter in baseball rarely exceeds a "300" batting average. But a "300" average is three times too low for a job-effective change agent! Fortunately, in the world of enterprise we usually have a reasonable amount of time. Poor evaluations that unleash undesirable changes are almost always built on either the shifting sands of an inadequate foundation of facts, or their overly hasty assessment. In the interest of getting a speedy result, we need to guard against the costly consequences of playing, "I can name that tune in two notes..."

Once we have mapped-out the best route, we can actually prepare and start on the beneficial change journey itself, or as we have termed it, the implementation phase. An adequate expenditure of time and effort must again be made if a real beneficial change is going to even begin to happen. Just as importantly, extended time in the form of "follow-up" is often essential to making sure a beneficial change actually does get, and stays implemented.

From Start To Finish Keep The Customer in Mind.

Figure 3.1 captures in diagram form the essence of the work process. There are several points worth emphasizing: First, while we have stressed in this chapter the gathering, evaluating, and activation aspects of the work process, its successful and efficient use is obviously dependent on a firm understanding of who is the customer, and what that customer wants. For, if we do not know where we are going it will not matter much how we get there!

Secondly, although the gathering, evaluating, and implementing steps are intended to be sequential, in the real world they are not necessarily unidirectional. Each succeeding step will often reveal some weaknesses in the preceding one. During the gathering phase we might well find ourselves still questioning the basic mission the customer expects to be completed. It needs to be clarified before moving on. During the evaluation phase some of the facts needed for a decision may be entirely missing or in conflict with each other. And even in the implementation phase it can happen that, for one reason or another, the proposed solution just isn't fully working out. So it is entirely possible, that despite a fair amount of care and diligence we may need to cycle back to an earlier step before any further progress can be made. In Figure 3.1 the feedback arrows are there to remind us of this point.

Lastly, no work process should be considered either finished or successful until the customer's agreement has been secured that the desired beneficial change has, indeed, been achieved. In other words we need a final sign off before claiming victory.

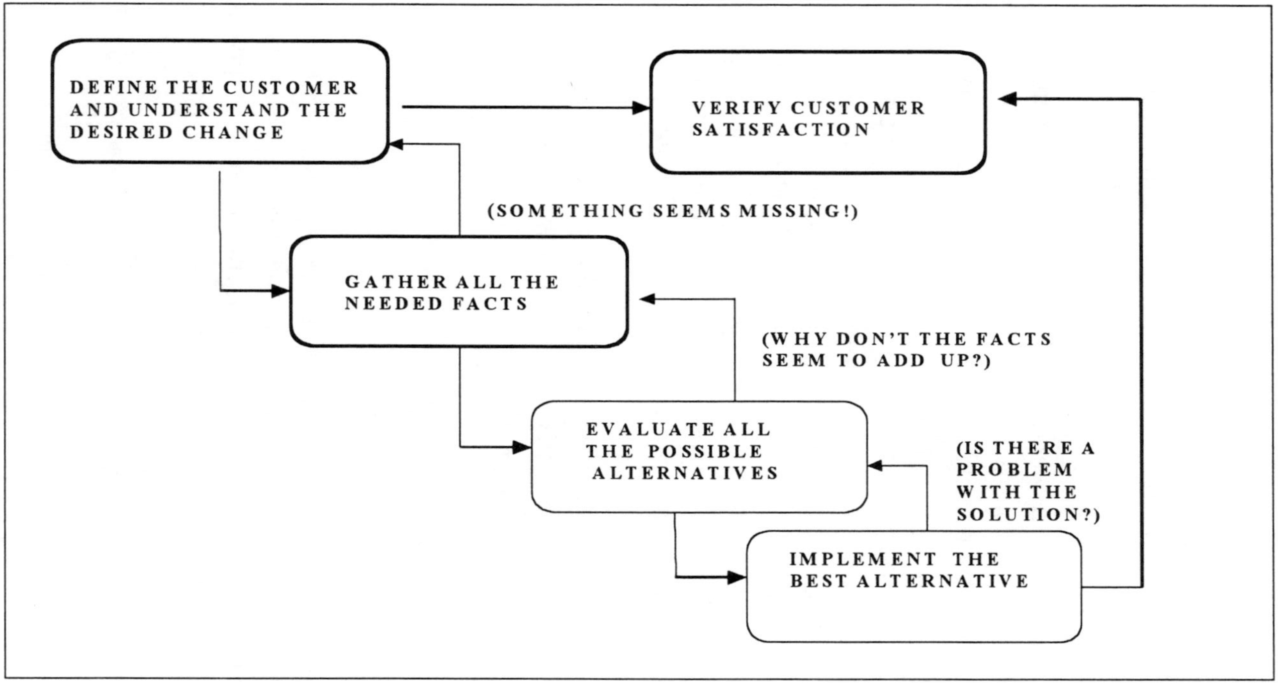

Figure 3.1 The Process Of Job-effective Work. (page 41)

One now humorous, although at the time painful example the writer can cite, where this did not happen, involved a new automotive product. I was part of a team that was asked by a major car manufacturer to come up with a new system that would communicate the status of various vehicle safety features to the driver. This next generation product was to replace the standard warning chimes and flashing lights that advise the driver that a door is not fully closed, a seat belt needs fastening, etc. After a lot of time and money spent defining the mission, gathering information worldwide, and evaluating various technical approaches, we came up with a solid state voice synthesis system that was able to advise and warn the motorist of nearly fifty different situations. We were especially proud of the quality of the artificial voice synthesis that seemed to duplicate a female pleasantly and faithfully.

Well, the big day arrived to demonstrate the system to the top executives, one of whom was a female marketing manager. No sooner had the first advisory been demonstrated when this lady exclaimed, "The last thing I would ever want in my car is another woman telling me how to drive!" So back to the drawing boards we went!

Who Are You Really Working For?

So far we have postulated that job-effective work means implementing customer-desired beneficial change, and that creating useful change follows a well-defined three-stage process: A process of gathering the needed information; evaluating that information in the form of the best possible alternative; and lastly translating that best alternative into action.

Shortly, we will take a look at several detailed examples of the change process. But there are still several sticky points with regard to customers that need to be dealt with. In examining the work process of the professional baseball player it is clear that his customers are his teammates, the fans, and the team owners. So, we have here a multiplicity of customers. And on further reflection we might very well add the player himself to the list, recognizing that his performance at the plate today is going to have at least some incremental impact on next year's salary negotiations. So, the first thing we want to keep in mind is that we will sometimes have several parties who have an interest in the same beneficial change. In this particular case, all of the customers have an identical interest in seeing that the player gets a hit.

But life is not always this simple; some of the people impacted by a change may well have divergent interests. Suppose your boss has been receiving a number of complaints from other department heads about frequently late and mis-delivered mail. One day he tells you to go down to the mailroom and "straighten things out." Now who is your customer? If we make use of our, "of benefit to a customer" concept, we are going to have to say that it is the other department heads. So what roles do your boss and the poor fellows who are going to being straightened-out play in this kind of situation? Well, we will say the boss is acting as a *sponsor* of the change and our mailroom friends are the *recipients* of the change.

Customers, sponsors, and recipients often have very different and even opposed interests. Beneficial change, like beauty, is always in the eyes of the beholder. It is no small part of the job-effectiveness task to sort out these various interests up front. In the corporate world, the military, academia, or for that matter, any large organization that breaks into departments or sub-groups, the divisive issue of customers, sponsors and recipients is bound to be with us. So, we must remember that for a job to be effective, we have to have at least one customer who gains a benefit. Sponsorship, which merely authorizes the change, will not do the trick.

Even worse is the not so rare change situation, where there is no customer, and only victimized recipients.

Agents of Change Are Good Advocates!

This brings us to a second potential stumbling block with the concept of beneficial change for a customer: there are lots of times when the proposed change, at that moment, may not seem all that desirable to the customer. For example, a physician advises a patient to undergo an operation with some serious risks, a lawyer advises his client to plead guilty or, in the more mundane realm, the Fuller Brush man tries to sell a homemaker a broom he or she may not want. So what do we do here? Well, we have to recognize that the first step is to gather customer support. A job-effective agent of change is a good advocate. The proposal has to be sold! And the way to make that happen, is to go back to our three-step change process and essentially make use of it twice. The first change we want is for the customer to have a different mindset. So we figure out the best approach to persuade the customer, and then we get that much behind us. Then, we use the change process again to perform the operation, enter the plea, or make the broom sale.

Also, it's rare that any worthwhile change is completely free of cost, inconvenience, or disruption. Doctors have a little saying that they tell to patients about the drugs they prescribe, "No side effects, no good effects!" Part of being a good advocate is to be able to honestly deal with these side effects in our selling job.

How Do You Like Your Spaghetti Cooked?

Many times we are going to be called upon in our jobs to implement a change, but we will have some nagging doubts about whether or not it is of real benefit to a customer. One, often useful way of sorting this out is to apply what we will call the "Q-B-C" test. There is a little, "mom and pop" Italian restaurant in South Philadelphia that has a sign hung-up on the wall by the order-counter. It is shown in Figure 3.2, and it neatly sums up a frequent dilemma for the change agent.

WOULD YOU LIKE YOUR SPAGHETTI……

….BETTER?
…..QUICKER?
…..CHEAPER?

PICK ANY TWO!!!!

Fig.3.2. Some Beneficial Changes Require Tough Choices

Much of our industrial progress in the form of new products and services can be explained in terms of a constant evolution of things that perform some function *quicker, better,* and/or *cheaper*. Ideally, we want our beneficial changes—our work products—to be all three. And if that is actually the situation we have come up with a real winner. More often, however, the proposed change is of such a benefit that it will suffice to provide an improvement in just one or two of these qualities, without going backwards, at least very far, on the other(s).

This situation calls for some real honest judgment on the part of the change agents, sponsors and customers. We need to make sure that our "spaghetti" warning sign can be clearly seen as they come in the door! There are an unbelievable number of ideas in the business world that seem pretty "beneficial" at first glance only to unleash total mayhem later on. Some hasty company re-organizations provide classic examples. In the inevitable post-mortems that are held they score very low on the "Q-B-C" test.

Does the following ancient quote regarding a re-organization sound timely and familiar?

"We trained hard, but it seemed that every time we were beginning to form into teams we would be reorganized. I was to learn later in life that we tend to meet any new situation by reorganizing, and what a wonderful method it can be for creating the illusion of progress while producing confusion, inefficiency, and demoralization"

Petronius Arbiter, 210 B.C.

Whether we are thinking of re-structuring the whole corporation or just changing the inter office mail-delivery pick up by ten minutes, thinking out the Q-B-C impacts ought to be a constant consideration.

Three Tries At Getting The Work Process Right.

Now we are ready for a few, concrete examples of the three-step change process. We will examine a purchase request that has been written poorly, and then a little better, before getting it right the third time. Suppose you were the boss and found on your desk the following memo:

Bob:
Re: Stamping Machine Purchase Request.

Please approve the attached requisition for $70,125 for a new stamping press that we absolutely need ASAP at the Johnstown plant.

If you have any questions, be sure to give me a call.

Bill

Based on that three-liner, there is little doubt that you are going to give Bill a short call to set-up a long meeting, before authorizing spending a little over seventy grand!

It also isn't likely that you would be in a big hurry to let the following "revised" request sail by:

Bob:

Re: Stamping Machine Purchase Request- Revised.

I hope this provides you with a little more of the detail you requested on the phone.

The present stamping press at the Johnstown plant is a nightmare to keep running. I have been meaning to get in touch with you for the last couple of weeks on this problem. We are lucky to be able to maintain 75% of the needed production rate for the valve line. Attached is a requisition for $70,125 for a new press that will get our capacity back to where it needs to be. Included in the purchase price are the costs for our operator training, some maintenance work and a pretty good offer for the old machine. John Ford knows the details of the maintenance agreement.

I know with the present profit pinch, we don't need this charge right now but I have to get the production out, especially for General Motors. We almost certainly put some money in the budget last year for redecorating that might be better used here. You can check with Susan in Accounting to see if we still have this money available.

Call me if you have any other questions. I really think its important that we get this requisition signed no later than tomorrow.

Bill

Bill's revised request is somewhat better than his original from the standpoint of the information supplied to make a reasonable decision to spend a substantial amount of money. But after we look at the third request, below, we are probably still going to classify the second request as a "bad-haircut."

Bob:
Re: Stamping Machine Purchase Request- 2nd Revision.

We have been having real trouble maintaining production volumes on the valve line at the Johnstown plant, without using a lot of expensive overtime. The basic problem is that the Acme stamping press, which is now over thirty years old can't be operated faster than 600 parts per hour. We need to be able to produce at least 800 parts per hour to meet GM's current needs. If we get the additional business we expect next year, we will have to be able to consistently hit 1100 parts per hour.

Besides the basic rate problem, we have had two major line shutdowns due to emergency repairs on the subject press. Last week we lost two full shifts because the main drive motor clutch burned-out. In April, we had to replace the lubrication pump, which again cost us a day's production run. I had the people in from Acme to talk about doing a complete overhaul on the press. It will cost in the range of twenty five thousand dollars, and of course we still will not have solved the limited capacity problem.

Acme's recommendation, to which I concur, is that we buy a new, Type EC-100 computerized stamping press for the valve line. Although the model they are suggesting costs

$89,125, they are offering a $19,000 rebate if we turn in the old press. The price also includes a five-year repair and maintenance agreement and one hundred hours of on-site operating training.

From a capacity standpoint, this press will handle 1500 parts per hour so we will have a 30% reserve beyond next year's expected volume increase.

I checked with Susan in Accounting and there still is $106,000 left in the maintenance budget for this year that was originally planned for building re-decorating. I think we can agree that it would be better to buy the press and defer some of the re-decorating plans to next year. I ran a payback analysis on the Acme proposal and it looks like with the increased production rate possible, we will recover our initial investment within thirty-one months. We will be able to save $18,000 annually just by eliminating the need to work overtime.

Attached is a requisition for $70,125, which takes into account the rebate on the old press. I would like you to give your approval. We can expect to have the press installed and operating four weeks after Acme receives the order.

You can reach me on extension 3098, if you need further information.

Thanks,

Bill

It is very useful to break apart or parse each of these three requests into the elements that fit under our three headings of gatherings, evaluations, and actions to be taken. In the first memo, we come up with one "fact" item, a purchase price of $70,125 for the press, which clearly belongs under the gathering column. Similarly Bill expressed one opinion, "We have an absolute need...." that we can place under the evaluation heading and, of course, one action, "Please approve...." Pretty slim pickings to base a seventy thousand-dollar decision on!

Bill's second memo requires a little more time to analyze. There is one solid fact for the gathering column, the purchase price, and what we might call a semi-fact buried in the thought "Included in the purchase price are the costs for our operator training, some maintenance work and a pretty good offer for the old machine."

If Bill is a whole lot shy on supporting facts, he makes up for it with at least six opinions starting with a "nightmare" and ending up with his "almost certain" faith that there must still be money in the budget. So it's six largely unsupported opinions that we have to put down in the "evaluations" column.

Finally there is only one action item—get the paperwork moving old buddy! Bill's second request not only is a "bad-haircut" piece of work from the gathering, evaluating and action standpoints, but also gives his boss some do-it-yourself hints that in case he is interested in something better, "John Ford has the details," and "You can check with Susan."

Now for Bill's third re-write: there are a total of 14 items, which can be reasonably regarded as solid facts that deal with:

1. Production capacities, current and needed.
2. Overhaul costs of the present press.
3. A breakdown of purchase price details for a new press.
4. Funds availability and payback on the investment of a new press.

Added all together this third set of comprehensive facts, which Bill has gathered provide a credible foundation for the major action items that he presents in the letter. It is easy for us to accept that a new press should be purchased instead of the old one being overhauled, and that the funds originally allocated for re-decorating of the building be used for this purpose. Notice how the evaluations in this instance present themselves in the form of buttressed recommendations rather than just unsupported opinions. If boss Bob accepts these two recommendations as presented, then they of themselves become the needed action items.

Practicing The Work Process With A Newspaper.

Analyzing any piece of work in terms of the elements that belong under gatherings, evaluations and actions can be very useful in developing a greater sense of job-effectiveness. But it does take a little practice to get the technique down right.

The daily newspaper is a great practice field. Just take a couple of editorials from the opinion page, a few replays from the sports page, and perhaps some advertisements. Begin by marking-off the supporting facts, evaluative opinions, and calls to action in each of these articles. After you have marked-up several different kinds of stories, take notice of the "fact" content of each, and how well these gatherings support the evaluations. Then, in turn, how well the evalautions buttress the expressed calls for actions to be undertaken.

Sports page articles are typically strong in the gathering phase; the myriad of statistics kept on each game provides a rich source of facts. Contrast this with the "Nine out of ten doctors ..." kinds of advertisements, and their quick leap to get the reader to act in the form of a purchase. Next find an editorial that you feel is really persuasive. Is it because the opinions expressed are easily derived from the facts presented? And is the bottom-line call for action a logical outcome of the evaluations offered?

Getting Some "Real World" Practice.

Once we have had some practice with news articles we can move into our own job-related, real world. Formal presentations, final reports, design reviews, case studies and even inter-office memos often provide excellent examples of work products intended for a customer. Each of these can be a case study of the basic steps underlying the beneficial change process.

The next time you are invited to listen to a coworker's presentation try taking notes by turning a sheet of paper sidewise, and listing the salient points under three side-by-side columns of gatherings, evaluations and calls for action. Chances are that you will find that it's a great way to make an assessment of the value of a work product to a customer. First look to see if a credible and comprehensive set of facts have been gathered by the presenter. Next, are the evaluations, which he or she has made consistent with these facts? Lastly, we want to know whether or not the recommended actions logically flow from the conclusions drawn.

A Job-Effective Work Process Builds A Pyramid.

As Figure 3.3 indicates, a truly beneficial work process reveals itself schematically as a well-defined pyramid. The base of the structure comprises the gatherings; the comprehensive and credible set of facts that form a broad foundation. At the mid-section of the pyramid are the evaluations; the carefully considered group of alternatives that we draw from the supporting facts. At the apex are the actions that must be implemented if the desired beneficial change is going to be accomplished. As a general rule, not only good presentations, but any job-effective piece of work collects a strong base of supporting facts. These considered facts, in turn, suggest a modest number of possible alternatives. A best course of action is then selected from the list of alternatives. Whenever a presentation or any other work product falls on its face, we will find they add up to some weird looking pyramids!

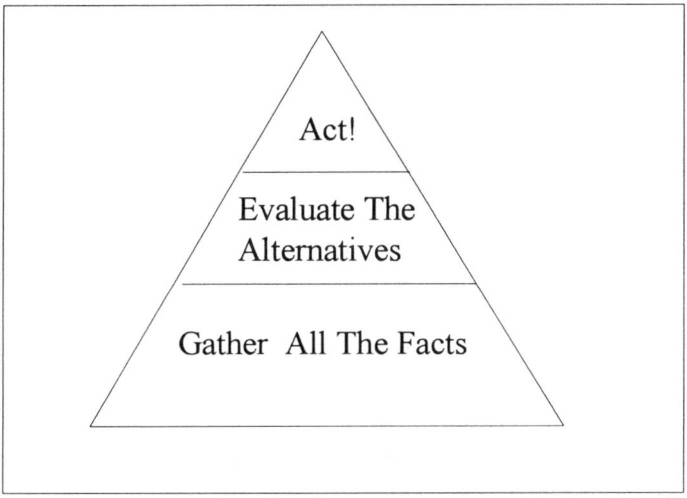

Figure 3.3. A Job-effective Work Process Builds A Solid Pyramid.

Two examples are represented by the first two purchase requests written by Bill. In the first memo, the pyramid has no solid gathering base. The single fact presented, namely the price of the press, has little to do with the evaluation made or the action to be taken. In the second memo, Bill is again short on supporting facts but tries to make-up for it by offering lots of evaluations in the form of personal opinions. His "pyramid" in this case would look more like a Christmas tree. Bill finally has it right on the third try, and if we diagram his memo it will indeed look like a pyramid.

Figure 3.4(a) shows schematically a change process that is only partially supported by the gathered facts. In time, the implemented change can be expected to collapse for lack of a stable foundation.

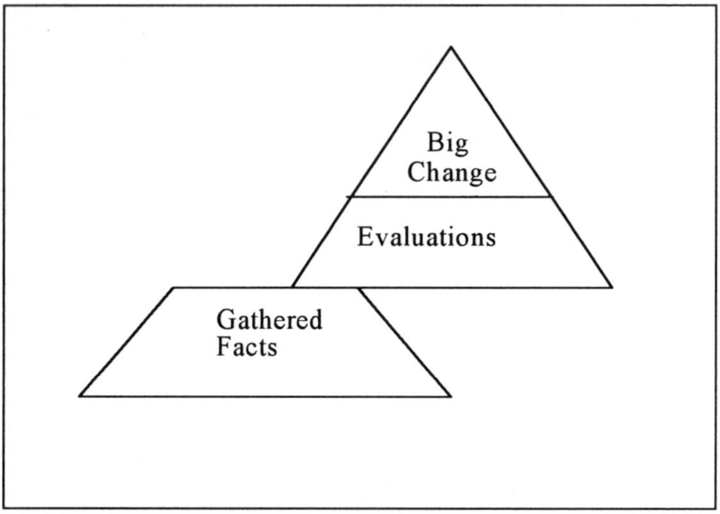

Figure 3.4(a). A Change Process Only Partially Supported By The Gathered Facts

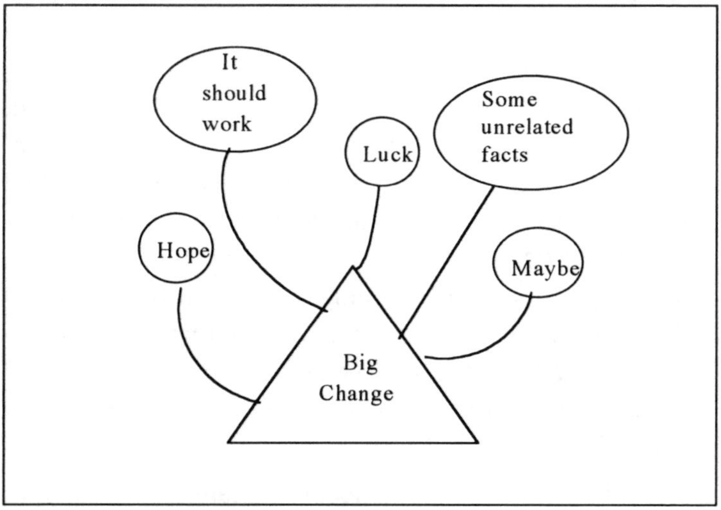

Figure 3.4(b). The "Hail Mary" Change Process

In Figure 3.4(b) there is no underlying foundation whatsoever, just a decision to act. In this latter case, the usual premise is, "We don't have time for all this gathering, and evaluation stuff!" It will be noted that the "Hail Mary" play is not something just seen in football!

The pyramid approach is a good litmus test for any customer-oriented work product. For example, some staff work efforts are extremely thorough in what is gathered and logically evaluated. But the work effort never culminates into meaningful action for want of an action-receptive customer. The work process pyramid never rises beyond a lopped-off trapezoidal stage. Many corporate offices have file drawers full of elaborate, trapezoidal plans.

When we really sit down and think about it, making any worthwhile change happen involves the three basic steps of gathering, evaluating, and acting. Here is a short list of non-work related activities that illustrates the point:

1. Preparing an income tax return.
2. Writing a book.
3. Planning a vacation.
4. Building a new house.
5. Buying a new car.

So why make a big deal about something we do all the time? The answer is simply that, although we do it all the time, we do not always do it well. Our inclinations are far more on the side of short-term personal success than long-term customer job-effectiveness. As a consequence, we try to see ten patients an hour instead of six, or we ship a dozen questionable parts instead of ten guaranteed good ones.

A Disturbing Measure of Job-Effectiveness.

Today, many corporations keep track of what is called their "Cost of Unquality." This figure measures the penalty costs associated with deficient products and services: basically the price that is paid for not doing a job right the first time. It covers everything from the costs of delayed introductions of new products, to charges for assembly line rework of current products on through liability costs of products long in the field. Shockingly, many quality experts put this cost in the range of twenty five to thirty percent of sales. This is about four times greater than typical bottom-line profits!

Looked at positively, the Cost of Unquality is a literal gold mine of opportunity for change agents! It is the wide-open playing field of the "turn-around" executive that is brought in to revitalize a foundering company.

However varied the sources of unquality costs may be, the underlying cause is always the same: somebody, at sometime, gave somebody else the job equivalent of a bad haircut! If we are going to change for the better, that is become consistently job-effective, then we need a consistent approach. The customer-focused, three-step, change process is intended to do just that.

A General's Viewpoint.

In a speech to management executives, General Colin Powell defined a leader as one, who:

1. Observes,
2. Thinks,
3. Plans, and then,
4. Acts with overwhelming force and passion.

Our three phase work process of gathering, evaluating, and implementing seems to fit well with the General's prescription for leadership. We observe all the relevant facts; think through the import of those observations; carefully plan out the best alternative action; and then translate that planned action into beneficial change. Of course, most of us do not have an army of troops or thousands of employees at our command to enact change. But we can still undertake the desired action with the needed "overwhelming force" in terms of the commitment, credibility, energy and follow-up we personally bring to the task. Chapter 4 will deal with those personal characteristics that foster a job-effective work process.

Summary.

All work aimed at achieving a beneficial result can be analyzed in terms of a three-step process. This process consists of gathering the needed facts regarding a proposed change; evaluating the best course of implementation required in order to create the desired change; and lastly, implementing the change. Beneficial changes are the result of sound evaluations. Credible evaluations are built on a solid foundation of facts. The agent of change always keeps in mind the differences between customers, sponsors, and recipients.

Discussion Problems.

1. Using some recent examples from your own work, school etc., "pyramid" diagram one good and one bad example of a change process. Count up the gatherings, evaluations, and actions for each. What impact did pre-selling of the beneficial change to the customer play in the outcome?

2. Surgeons, airline pilots, and policemen often have to take actions of great consequence in a very few seconds. How can they effectively use the three-phase change process?

3. List out the beneficial change, the customers, sponsors, and recipients for five of your recent work efforts.

4. Give three recent job assignments where the objective of the change was to do something quicker, better, or cheaper.

5. Your sponsor and your customer are in strong agreement that a change, which you have proposed, should be implemented as soon as possible. However, word gets back to you that some of the recipients are "dead-set" against the idea. What is your next move?

6. Your company is engaged in the manufacture of small kitchen appliances— coffee makers, toasters etc. You are requested to do a market study on opportunities for these products in Brazil. You are given three months to complete this study, at which time you will be expected to make a detailed presentation on your findings to the senior management. For each of the following steps in the overall work process list the tasks you intend to pursue, and the amount of time you will budget to each:

   a) Defining the customer desired change.
   b) Gathering information.
   c) Evaluating alternatives.
   d) Developing an action plan.
   e) Preparing a management presentation.

Chapter 4—A Sixpack of Job Attributes

Discovering The Vital Personal Ingredients Of Job-Effectiveness

In the two previous chapters we focused on *approach*—what we mean by job effective work, and the systematic manner by which we make it happen. Now we want to take a look at how *attitude* interweaves with approach in the make up of the fabric of today's change agent. In particular, we want to take a close look at each of the threads that form the repeating pattern of this attitude "warp".

We want to ask ourselves what are the personal qualities that will enable us to consistently perform effectively that three phase task we call work. Ideally, we would like to identify a handful of attributes, which really serve to define a job-effective person in today's very dynamic and demanding working world. Here, we come up with a bit of a problem. As the partial list of Table 4.1 suggests, there are dozens of personal characteristics that each of us has observed among people, whom we consider to be outstanding job performers. So, it takes a little discernment to settle on those that truly are the *sine qua non* of job-effectiveness.

Working Styles.

One way we can begin to pare down this list is to recognize that some of these qualities like honesty and fairness towards others really relate to our basic sense of

Good Listener	Persevering	Mature	Analytical
Confident	Well Organized	Flexible	Inspiring
Open Minded	Consistent	Patient	Loyal
Resourceful	Decisive	Approachable	Fair Minded
High Initiative	Charismatic	Caring	Demanding
Credible	Dedicated	Precise	Aggressive
Honest	Hard Working	Results Oriented	Committed
Engaging	Down-to-earth	Energetic	Good Follow Up
Thorough	Quick Learn	Disciplined	Punctual
Visionary	Team Player	Risk Taker	Responsible

Table 4.1. Some Of The Many Attributes Frequently Associated With Job-effective Workers. (page 60)

personal morality. Good morals are both necessary and beneficial to the long- term success of the business. The many job issues relating to race discrimination and sexual harassment over the last thirty years have unmistakably demonstrated this fact. But while being a moral person is a necessary condition, it alone is hardly sufficient for us to consider ourselves as being job-effective.

There is a second grouping of qualities we can form from our original list of high performance attributes. These qualities relate to what we might call working styles. Being well organized, articulate, and punctual are some examples of working styles. The importance and appropriateness of particular work styles varies with the job and circumstances. We would like members of our sales team to be aggressive but not our clergyman. On the other hand, both need to be approachable. Military leaders must often be demanding in the extreme sense, while the remedial education teacher may need an abundance of patience. We like working for a boss who is a gifted speaker, but we have all seen leaders who come across a bit wooden, yet are consistently very effective at getting a job done. No one enjoys working with an arrogant individual, but this is not to deny that the work output of these "jerks" is often so good that people learn to work around them.

Thus, positive working styles, while not the essence of job effectiveness, serve to lubricate the entire work process, just as negative styles create unnecessary friction. As such we want to include as many of these positive qualities in our toolbox as possible. In organizations where particular work styles tend to be widely shared they create an identifiable culture that can be a powerful support system for the objectives of the business. For example, the culture and, for that matter, the language in a truck assembly plant is decidedly different than that of, say, the main public library.

But then again getting a truck assembly line back on schedule is a lot different than dealing with an overdue book.

Essential Work Attributes.

Having separated out basic morals and desirable working styles, we can now begin to narrow down our search for the essential and defining attributes of job-effectiveness. The answer is to be found in our job mission. Early in this book we defined our overall mission as being an agent of change. So we need to ask ourselves what are the key qualities of an effective change agent? Experience tells us that:

1. Nobody begins to institute change without taking the *initiative.*
2. Nobody gets the vital support of others to make change happen without *personal credibility.*
3. Nothing significant changes without the expenditure of considerable physical and mental *energy.*
4. Nobody can be an effective agent of change in today's ever-changing business environment without a high degree of *self-adaptability.*
5. Nobody can keep change moving forward to a successful conclusion without an abiding sense of *commitment.*
6. Nothing stays changed without disciplined *follow-up.*

Collectively, we will refer to these six particular attributes as our job-effective work ethic. Now a fair question is, "How do we know these are the right six?" Might there really be five or seven? Well, the truthful answer is we can't be absolutely sure! We can only go by experience and do a "sanity check" on our suppositions. Our experience may end up making us think that the earth is flat, but if our conclusions are supported by all the available data that is the best we can do. After all, aside from the stone-carved Ten

Commandments, our everyday laws, rules, and guidelines are the simple products of time-tested experience.

In the following pages and in some of the discussion problems at the end of the chapter, we will attempt to develop a detailed rationale for including each of these six attributes. But up front we can agree that job-effectiveness has everything to do with how we are inclined to use our hearts, minds, and bodies to make customer-desired beneficial change happen. Certainly, those six traits of the work ethic relate intimately to those three vital elements of our being.

****

Key Attribute #1- Initiative.

At Sears they like to talk about their "die-hard" batteries, but really it is the automobile's electric starting motor that should get the lion's share of the credit! Perhaps, you have escaped the misfortune of having your car's starter drop dead on you. If so, you ought to know that the biggest and finest V-8 in the world will get you nowhere, without being brought to life with a good, reliable starter. Nobody's jumper cables will get you past a bad starter. It either works or you get towed!

The development of the electric starter motor is one of the great, but now-forgotten achievements of automotive history. It eluded the mechanical genius of Henry Ford and his engineers for twenty years. So, when Charles "Boss" Kettering came up with a workable solution in 1912, it was heralded as a seminal event by the motoring public. This innovation did much to launch General Motors along the road of becoming a corporate giant. Before then car engines had to be started using a hand crank. This was an exhausting, time-consuming, and sometimes dangerous task that kept hospitals filled with wrenched backs, broken arms, and not a few heart attacks.

The starter motor is a very specialized device because it has to pack a lot of power in a small package about the size of a two-quart, tin can. Getting a two hundred horsepower engine to turn-over on a sub-zero day is a tough, tough job!

We can think of personal initiative as the starting motor of any process of beneficial change. It is key for the agent of change, because even though lots of people in an organization are powered by some pretty energetic V-8's, and can do lots of work, they don't always come with a hefty enough starter motor that will get them moving in the first place.

Did you ever try to move a heavy piece of furniture, say, a dresser, across the floor? If you did, you probably had the sensation that it was doubly hard to get the piece of furniture moving in the beginning. Once it started to move it seemed much easier. You were not just imagining this, there is a well-known physical reason why this is so: non-moving or static friction tends to be a lot greater than sliding friction. And when we humans want to get our hearts, minds, and bodies moving in a certain direction, we also tend to offer the most resistance right up front. How many times have we experienced that the worst part of doing some needed home chore is getting up off the sofa?

So we can think of initiative as that up front burst of insight and enthusiasm that sees the opportunity for beneficial change and the willingness to get the organizational V-8 moving in the direction to make it happen.

Change Means Risk Taking.

Of course any significant change when first proposed has an attendant risk; it could very well fail! Especially at the beginning of a project, what we don't know *is* precisely what we don't know! Moreover, in the case of a large organization there are likely to be, as noted earlier, some perceived undesirable side effects. Side effects that will generate varying degrees of resistance, at least on the part of some people. Initiative gives us not only the confidence to personally bet on a successful outcome, but along with commitment the fortitude to deal with the expected resistance.

Initiative comes in many guises: If you are an engineer who shows a lot of initiative, people will say that you are innovative; salesmen who take the initiative are considered aggressive in an admired sense, while politicians willing to venture into something new are thought to be progressive. Finally, business leaders in this situation are considered to be dynamic. But no matter what the accolade, it all comes down to a change agent seeing an opportunity to make a positive change, and the willingness to take a measured personal risk.

Sam's Different Idea.

Initiative is vision expressed in action. Sam Walton, Wal-Mart's founder, is a good example of this concept. Sam was certainly not the first to think-up the idea of superstores with everyday low prices. That business model has been around for a long time! But he did have the critical insight that it could be made to work in the thousands of small towns and farm communities that the other discounters had assiduously avoided. Like it or not, he singularly understood that rural America would be willing to break life-long habits of patronizing small Main street shops and drive to the big gray-blue box on the edge of town, just so long as the prices were right.

Sam translated this vision into a life-long stream of initiatives of jawboning suppliers, pleading with bankers, exhorting employee "associates" and cajoling community zoning boards, as he built his empire one store at a time. Few would claim that the Wal Mart phenomenon is an unmixed blessing. But today, with 140 billion dollars in annual sales and a payroll of some 800,000 employees, it does stand as a monument to one man's initiative!

****

Key Attribute #2 - Personal Credibility

If initiative is a measure of the willingness of someone to take a risk to bring about a beneficial change, then credibility is a measure of the willingness on the part of everyone else to support the change agent in the pursuit of that idea. One grants to himself as much initiative as he wishes. But credibility is a gift from others, only reluctantly bestowed, and then in only small measures. It is therefore the most precious attribute of the job-effective work ethic, always to be treasured, and never to be squandered on a half-baked idea.

Every change involves the risk of failure. Risk not only to the one who initiates the change but often of wider consequence to those who are impacted downstream. For this reason change tends to be resisted, even when a currently undesirable situation is clearly perceived. There is an old saying, "Far better to deal with a devil you know than one you have never met before!" High personal credibility is the most powerful antidote for organizational resistance to change.

How Is Our Organizational Credit Rating?

Most of us have had the experience of going to a bank in order to apply for a home mortgage. From filling out the mounds of paperwork that goes with a mortgage application, we know that the bank was interested in two things: complete details on the property we were buying, and our long-term financial ability to repay the loan. Almost certainly the bank had the property independently appraised, and also did a detailed check on our repayment track record of previous borrowings. The lending institution was looking for some reassurance that it was not taking on an undue risk.

In the work-a-day world, implementing change successfully almost always depends on the support of others. At the very least, we will need our coworkers' acquiescence. More likely, we will need a real investment of their time and effort. Occasionally, it might even mean a risk to their reputations or careers. So, like the bank, our superiors and coworkers will try to minimize these risks by an unspoken, but rather thorough, up front "credibility-check," each time we take on the role of change agent.

A first step of this assessment is the basic credibility of the change idea that we propose. It's like appraising the house we wanted to buy. Customers, sponsors, and recipients alike are going to want to know if the beneficial change seems like a smart or a crazy idea; or is it somehow threatening with unforeseen side effects. But like the bank loan this counts for only half of the risk assessment. Just as important are our perceived abilities to make this change happen, based on our past track records. All of us have met walking suggestion boxes that spout out a continuous stream of "we oughta's...." but in the end change nothing. So, coworkers have a natural concern for an individual's ability to carry a job all the way through.

Thus, we have to keep in mind that the personal credibility factor in implementing a change has two vital parts: the credibility of the idea itself, and the credibility of the initiator to make it happen.

The Instant Credit Check.

There are two important dimensions to the credibility of the initiator; one we will call "sight" credibility and the other "earned" credibility. Sight credibility is the way our colleagues perform an instant credit check on us as initiators. Like the bank, we all want to know everything we can about someone who could make a change that might affect us. But unlike the bank we usually don't have the time, the power, or the resources. So we do the next best thing: we take a quick look, have a short listen, and then make some very long inferences about the initiator.

These look and listen input signals come in infinite variety; his tone of voice and wingtip shoes, or her hairstyle and European accent. Even more fascinating are the varieties of possible, inferential outputs! Some of us might find his voice to be commanding, but in the same presentation consider her to be "pushy." We think gray hair is a plus for the VP of Finance, but a negative for an entry-level accountant. We feel people are odd-balls, who wear pin-stripped suits in Silicon Valley, but we feel just the same about those who show up at the New York office wearing a sports shirt. We believe that being over six feet is the sign of a natural born leader, but those managers under five foot eight tend to be "Naopoleonic." And on and on go are instant credit stereotypical assessments.

Checking Our Own Instant Credit.

Everyone agrees it is not a very good system, but until we humans evolve to the point where we can directly read the minds of other people, this is the way we are going to be inclined to make our instant credit checks. Because of this, each of us is a Rorschach inkblot test; others will tend to see in us what they want. The important point to recognize is that each of us has plus and minus instant credit signals that we transmit to others. And most times if we are honest with ourselves we will know precisely what they are.

So, the first thing we want to do is to list all our plus signals on one side of a paper. Typically these might number about a half dozen. Our job with these is easy; just be thankful every time we think about them.

Next, we want to write down each of our negative instant–credit signals. Again there are probably about a half dozen that cover the spectrum from trivial to major. Our task is to study that list hard, and resolve that we are going to bring most of those negatives into neutral territory, and actually turn a few into positives. It may be as easy as buying a new wardrobe that matches the culture of our work environment, or as time consuming as eliminating a distracting mannerism.

There may be one item on the negative list for which we, or perhaps those around us, are convinced that we can do absolutely nothing. Take a closer look at this seeming impediment; maybe we can turn it into a super-plus! What is a super-plus? Well, it is little kids in leg braces who grow up to win "the Gold" at the Olympics; stutters who become the nightly news anchor; and rebelliously poor students who go on to become another Winston Churchill.

A Blind Man At A Chalkboard.

When I was starting my career, I had to take a company-required seminar on the systems design of computers. In other words, how the computer's memory links up with the processor that actually does the computing; how these in turn are tied to the keyboard and printers; and how the data is moved back and forth etc. At the start of the seminar, I noticed upon taking my seat near the back of the room that the instructor was wearing dark glasses, and that he held his head in an odd, mostly-fixed position, even as he talked and paced across the front of the classroom. Sensing my growing curiosity, a man beside me, leaned over and whispered "He's blind!" No sooner had I heard this, when the instructor turned to the blackboard behind him, reached for a piece of chalk, and began to draw a computer "systems" diagram.

First he drew a box, called it the arithmetic unit, and somehow managed to write that label very nearly in the center of the box. Next, he turned back to the class and commented for a few minutes on the specific functions of the arithmetic unit. He repeated the same process for the memory unit, choosing a space on the board to the right of the arithmetic unit. Then, in turn, he did the same for the keyboard, and each of the other so-called "peripherals," until finally, he had the elements of a whole computer spread across the board.

As the process unfolded there were growing smiles and chuckles throughout that room. The boxes were reasonably square and spaced out quite evenly. Somebody behind me kept muttering over and over again, "How the hell can he do that?" But the best was still to come! The teacher began to "'wire-up" the computer, correctly drawing dozens of criss-crossing lines between the different boxes and not missing a one. As he finished these inter-connections the class erupted in an amused applause. But only the tiniest of grins crossed the instructor's face. Once again, he faced the class and said in a sly manner, "Well, before we move on, do you have any questions," pausing a moment while his sightless eyes swept the room, "on just how a *computer* works?"

In my engineering career I have looked at thousands of such diagrams, ninety-nine percent of which I promptly forgot. But thirty-five years later I can still see that computer system on the board because it was created by a man with a "super plus"! And thirty-five years later I occasionally wonder to myself, "How in the world did he do that?"

All of us have met spellbinding public speakers. These are the same people who are most likely to tell us of an early shyness, painful awkwardness, or paralyzing stage fright that took them years to overcome. It was their opportunity to build a super-plus. If you need a little motivation to get working towards a super-plus, just imagine yourself six months, a year from now, or whatever it takes doing that "can-do-nothing-about" negative so effectively that the people around you start muttering to themselves, "How the heck can he do that so well!"

Earned Credibility.

Sight credibility can be extremely important whenever we first meet someone. All of us learn this lesson the first time we nervously ask that special girl we just met to the Junior Prom, or apply for our first job. But once we have been into a job or relationship for any length of time, the credibility factor takes on a very different shape. People now start to evaluate us based on a much more solid kind of evidence: our credibility track record. They will compare everything we did against everything we promised, as long as they have known us. We are going to refer to that track record as our earned credibility.

Our work associates will use this accumulated credibility, as the major predictor of future performance. Pick up today's newspaper and you are going to find that public acceptance or rejection of today's choices for a prestige coaching position, a Fortune 100 executive position, or the appointment of a high government official, all hinge on their established track records. On a less grand scale, the same approval process will come into play in ratifying the selection of the night shift line foreman, or even the chairperson for the company picnic.

So how do we build up our earned credibility? The answer has to be like the Smith Barney commercial on how they earn their money—"The old fashioned way. Slowly!" For true job-effectiveness, unquestioned honesty, a passion for getting all the facts down correctly, and a reputation for careful preparation are those old-fashioned starting ingredients. Then, comes the telltale follow-up process of finishing the job we said we would.

Dean Witter, a competitor of Smith Barney, likes to talk about "measuring success one investor at at time." We can also learn something from them; for job-effectiveness, we earn our credibility one customer at a time! Therefore, all other things being equal, longevity in an organization ought to be an advantage. Everything significant we do at work gets stored in the organization's memory bank, and like a good financial investment, compounds over time.

One Man's Credibility.

The near collapse and impending bankruptcy of Chrysler in 1980 shocked and in some ways saddened much of America. What family did not, at one time, own a Plymouth, have a Dad who talked endlessly about his 1955 De Soto, or hoped someday to own an eye-catching New Yorker. It should not have come as a surprise—Chrysler had a decades long, continuous down-hill slide. Once outselling even Ford in the 1930's, its market share had declined to about 20 percent in the early 1950's. By 1980 it had further dropped to well under 10 percent. At this point it simply no longer had the "critical mass" needed for survival.

Chrysler did have one thing going for it though: a new president in the personage of Lee Iacocca, best known as the father of the hugely popular Mustang and the classy Mark III. From his early years as a Ford management trainee Iacocca had developed a sterling reputation "to deliver," as they like to say it around Detroit. This notwithstanding, Lee had recently lost his presidential job at Ford for having apparently made Henry Ford II feel uncomfortably jealous about his headline-stealing showmanship. But a tour-de-force in credibility, delivered with showmanship, was precisely what Chrysler needed. And the chance to avenge the stinging hurt to a rough-edged but proud man, at the peak of his career, was exactly what Lee Iacocca needed at that moment. Thus, he wasted no time in his mission to resurrect Chrysler from among the near dead with his best-honed credibility tool—personal persuasion. First, Iacocca successfully persuaded the US government to guarantee $1.5 billion in loans to keep the company temporarily afloat. An unsecured amount so large that it raised qualms within the US Congress.

Next, he pushed hard on Chrysler's thousands of employees, already weary from a decade of downsizings, to work even harder, and in some cases at reduced pay. Chrysler's legion of suppliers were similarly asked, and if necessary arm-twisted, into price reductions and extending credit. Lastly, in thousands of TV ads Iacocca flawlessly played, for years, the folksy salesman. He sold all America hard on the less than obvious performance capabilities and hidden charms of the small, boxy "K-cars."

We know the outcome. The government loan was fully paid back three years after receiving it. And the "new" Chrysler Corporation became known and studied for its ability to react faster than its competitors. It was the first company to introduce the extremely popular minivans in 1984. Then, came the Jeep Grand Cherokee as the continuing fashion statement of the nineties. The Jeep was followed by a succession of rakish sedans later on. Who could have imagined in 1980 that the trend-setting and prestigious Daimler Benz organization would someday woo tired-old Chrysler into its worldwide fold? Surely, thousands of talented and dedicated individuals helped turn around Chrysler. But the point is they would have never had the opportunity without one man's credibility to deliver!

****

Key Attribute #3 – Personal Energy.

We marvel at the wonders our high tech culture has introduced to the market place over the last twenty years: laptop computers, the Internet, lasers, gene engineering and wireless communications to name just a few. What is just as amazing, however, is the enormous speed by which new competitors, with improved generations of these technologies, are able to capture market share by increasing performance or lowering costs. For example, through a continuous stream of technological advancements, the basic information processing capability of semiconductors has doubled every eighteen months, with predictable regularity. So predictable that it is known as Moore's Law, after the man who first postulated it. This law literally sets the pace in a never-ending, worldwide race among semiconductor manufacturers.

But "time to market" is not only a high tech phenomenon! From the standpoint of merchandise carried, the store lines of Wal Mart are not a whole lot different than that of, say, Sears or K Mart. Yet Wal Mart quickly outdistanced these long-established competitors. How is this so? It is because they developed a system of having the right products, in the right stores, and in the right quantities, faster than anyone else. In this sense, "low-tech" Wal Mart's secret of success is exactly the same as "high-tech" Dell Computer.

Speed of response, as measured by time to market, is the definitive weapon in today's hyper-competitive world. And an organization that runs at top speed does so, simply because there are a lot of high-energy people pushing it along. Thus, the agent of change needs to be both an energetic, and an energizing individual.

Unfortunately, our individual energy capacities are in some measure determined by our bodily constitutions. Mother Nature does not always distribute this gift fairly at birth, or evenly as life proceeds. So, not everybody can be a "jock";

get by with five hours sleep a night; or take the stairs two at a time, all the time. But there is a lot we can do to maximize our physical energy capacities from taking vitamins to pumping iron several days each week at the local gym. Job-effectiveness, therefore, demands that we wisely use and maintain the physical energy store we have been allotted.

Effort: Energy That Is Mentally Disciplined.

Just looking at the physical side of our energy output, however, ignores an important aspect of the work process: some job tasks are a lot more demanding in terms of the mental energy required. Sometimes we don't have very good tools to use; a job may be exceptionally boring, or perhaps, tedious and complex. At other times, we may encounter a lot of resistance from others in completing a task. Just as often, it is our own self-resistance. After all attention deficit disorder is not just for kids! So, we note there is a second dimension to our working energy, which we refer to as "effort." *Effort is mentally disciplined energy;* a sense of determination to see a task completed.

We know that the root source of our earthly physical energy is sunlight. Yet because it is so diffused, ordinarily it affects us little more personally than an occasional beach sunburn. But if you ever took a simple magnifying glass, and focused those same sun rays to a point on a piece of paper, you know you can cause the paper to ignite. Just as the magnifying glass harnesses the power of the sun, so it is with mental effort. It allows us to focus our store of work energy where it can do the most good.

We often hear that we should work smarter and harder. Disciplined effort, which is a trait that resides in our wills, is the smart way of working hard. Along with commitment that makes its home in our hearts, effort is what allows us to see a job through in its totality. As such, effort knows that a long climb, which typifies many a work process, is best accomplished one step at a time. It is an acquired gift, and as such, often comes a little later in life as we gain experience. Many a person, whose physical stamina is limited, has found an answer to job-effectiveness in the story of the hare and tortoise. They can more than make up for the physical energy shortage with some carefully focused and sustained effort.

The Energy and Effort of Michelangelo.

Perhaps, the greatest artistic talent of all times is Michelangelo. Four hundred years later we still stand in awe of his interpretive inspiration and technical skill. So much so that we tend to overlook the tremendous energy and sense of effort that drove this rare talent.

Just consider the energy and effort that went into his masterpiece, the ceiling panorama of the Vatican's vaulted Sistine chapel. Michelangelo labored on this work which covers over 10,000 square feet for over four and one half years. That averages out to about eight square feet of painted surface per day—a real sustained effort! But that is only the beginning of the story. The entire work was created by employing a difficult, wet plaster, fresco technique. A difficulty that was infinitely compounded by the need to paint hundreds of intricate figures while he lay on his back, seventy feet above the floor, in dim candlelight.

The noted historian Will Durant summed up the life of this extraordinary artist, sculptor, and architect in this way:

"It was first of all energy, a wild consuming force that tortured Michaelangelo's body, but sustained it for eighty nine years, and second a power of will that kept that energy harnessed and directed to one purpose—Art—ignoring almost everything else. Now energy directed by a unifying will is almost a definition of genius."[8]

How Much Time On The Job Is Really Enough?

There is an overriding question that relates to energy and effort. It is one that has very much come to the forefront as a result of the 1990's downsizing efforts of many corporations, and the general effects of global competition. How much time should a job-effective individual be willing to devote to his or her job? All of us are asked to do more each day, which can easily translate itself into an insatiable demand for more and more hours on the job. Each of us needs to come to terms with this demand as to whether we work forty, fifty, or seventy hours per week based on our own individual job responsibilities, compensation, and long-term aspirations. The following may set some helpful guidelines:

1. In our globally competitive and fast-changing world of enterprise we need to work *hard*, if we are going to be successful, and our organization is going to thrive. A job-effective worker should willingly respond to a rush-job, or a crisis situation, for his or her employer when needed. Unforeseen problems occur in every business setting. Likewise, some attractive opportunities with customers have narrow time windows for response. However, an operation that finds itself in a constant "crisis-du-jour" mode more than likely needs better leadership, rather than more self-sacrificing employees.

2. Time spent on the job must be calibrated two dimensionally in terms of the relative physical and mental energies that are put forth. Job-effectiveness has a decided "quality-time" aspect. This is the *smarter* side of work. It cannot be measured fairly in terms of a strict accounting of behind-the-desk hours per week.

3. During the late eighties and early nineties many employees suffered "burn-out" on the job through

relentless overwork. Their recovery from a zombie-like, depressed state was slow and partial, if at all. Their accumulated rewards were meager, if at all.

4. A job-effective worker is not the same as a job-addicted worker. Nor, is he or she the office martyr. A job is one of the vital paths we travel as we journey through life. It is not life's destination!

Dealing With Energy Robbing Issues.

There is one last aspect related to our personal energy conservation that also needs to be taken into account. Although our overriding interest is our on-the-job performance, our energy and effort demands run round the clock. Financial difficulties, family illnesses, kids' school problems, and martial difficulties all drain our energies and challenge our abilities to focus on purposeful work efforts.

Once again, Life does not seem to hand out these burdens with any apparent degree of fairness. Answers to these kinds of problems are hardly within the scope of this book. Suffice to say that sometimes the most dramatic improvements in job-effectiveness come from seeking good professional help for these home problems. It may also be not totally out of place to observe that those who are fortunate enough to have some spiritual connection with a "Higher Power" seem to come to a workable resolution the quickest.

****

Key Attribute #4-Self Adaptability.

In the first chapter we reviewed the many changes taking place in the world of enterprise. We found that we now work in a world of accelerating change; some would say chaotic change. Change brought about by new business models: retail stores give way to department stores; department stores lose out to discounters; discounters to speciality stores; speciality stores to super stores. We thought Wal Mart was the end of the line. But then came on-line shopping. What is next?

Technology brings about enormous change: productivity enhancing computers destroy thousands of routine-based jobs, while at the same time they open up much more creative jobs for thousands more. Jet airplanes bring us in contact with the remotest reaches of the world in a matter of hours. Wireless communication does it in milliseconds. Letters succumb to fax machines only to be replaced by "e-mail." Sensor-laden microprocessors check on patients in intensive care, and lasers replace scalpels.

Changing life styles also create changing business opportunities: big gas-guzzling sedans are replaced by small cars; vans obsolete small cars; soccer moms switch from cavernous vans to trucky SUV's. What will people want to drive next?

Global competition creates change; we now lose the business to a faceless company in Indonesia or Brazil, not the well- known competitor on the other side of town.

Change may be the ultimate paradox! We humans have become gifted engineers in creating change through new business models, a flood of next generation technologies, world-wide competition, and an endless parade of new products. We applaud these changes that seem to touch us, for the most part, positively and peripherally. But we are not nearly so comfortable with a new working ethic. For here, we are not changing things or systems. Rather we must be prepared to re-engineer ourselves.

To cope with all these changes, we, the workers, must change. More precisely, we need to constantly self-adapt. In today's world of enterprise we have two months to learn a foreign language; we must get used to holding midnight teleconferences with the Japanese office three nights in a row; and be prepared to revamp this year's profit plan several times in one quarter. How we work, and with whom we work, continues to change. More and more we find women in the executive suite, in the cockpits, and on the fire trucks. The open door policy is no more, now it is the wall-less office. Maybe the office is wherever we happen to find a place to plug in our laptop, and casual dress is no longer just on Fridays.

A Lesson From Sophomore Biology.

In sophomore biology we slowly learn about and quickly forget an important concept–homeostasis. Like all living beings our bodies comprise vast and sophisticated systems to maintain a state of equilibrium. Systems, for example, that keep our body temperature constant over wide environmental changes and the complex composition of our body fluids chemically precise. Homeostasis is built into ever cell of our bodies. It is not surprising, then, that it spills over into our mental processes.

It has been demonstrated that a normally skittish frog will unresponsively allow itself to be boiled alive, provided only that the water temperature be raised very slowly. Here is the Achilles heel of the otherwise vital homeostasis: dramatic changes taking place over relatively long periods of time, tend to be ignored.

So it is with us. It is difficult to keep track of the pennies of change that are relentlessly adding up to costly dollars. We ignore a cold until it becomes the "flu"; we tolerate the flu until it becomes pneumonia. We blindly inch our way towards the financial cliffs one new credit card at a time. So too at work! For a long while we seem able to "get by" without learning to use a computer, updating our sales presentations, or healing a rocky relationship with a colleague. But surely the day comes when we get laid-off, lose a valued customer or don't get a long sought promotion. Like the frog, we find ourselves unwittingly boiled alive!

Organizational Homeostasis.

Organizations, being made up of homeostatic-comfortable people are no less vulnerable. Generals famously train armies with tactics and equipment used to fight the last war; churches and unions silently watch memberships slowly erode over decades; governments keep in place long failed welfare policies. Organizational change, like self-change, is often viewed as being too painful!

The tendency of an enterprise to hang on to obsolete products is illustrative. Studies show that three out of four displacing product innovations come from outside the companies, which established the product market in the first place.[9] More telling, the same studies show that, in the vast majority of cases, the original companies failed to self adapt despite having a clear understanding of the need for an updated product, and an early view of their soon-to-be competitors intentions. The literature cites abundant examples: Sailing ships displaced by steam ships; mechanical typewriters obsoleted by electric typewriters; and electrics made useless by word processors. Similarly, it took only twenty-five years for the tiny transistor to replace the bulbous vacuum tube; even less time for the discrete transistor to succumb to the integrated circuit.

On the other hand, many companies, well populated with agents of change, have been able to make market and technological changes consistently a wellspring of opportunity rather than a treacherous pit. Motorola is an outstanding example of this ability to organizationally adapt over the better part of the twentieth century. Beginning with a simple battery supply for the first car radios of the 1930's they migrated their skills to car radios themselves. By 1960 they had a large share of the television set market. Exiting that business as it peaked, they found successive waves of opportunities in mobile communications, semi-conductors, automotive electronics, and cell phones. Today, they are pioneering satellite communications. And the results through 1999? Sales of $30 billion annually and 150,000 employees around the globe. Not bad, for two brothers starting in a Chicago back-alley garage with a single product idea! Hewlett Packard, Rubber Maid, and Merck are other examples, where the continual innovations brought about by perceptive change agents have led to similarly rewarding growth.

Self-Adaptability: The Change Agents Signature Attribute.

Self-adaptability, the ability to appropriately change personally to meet emerging organizational needs, is the signature attribute of the job-effective change agent in the new millennium. It is has become the brightest star in the job-effectiveness galaxy. But for many of us, it remains the most distant. It is hard to terminate a project which we have sold hard, and in which we have invested so much time, credibility, and personal commitment. It becomes only a little more easy because the evidence clearly suggests there is a better opportunity waiting.

It is hard to adapt to a flattened organization when we have already spent half a job-lifetime moving up the organizational ladder one slow rung at a time. Even if we ourselves perceive the pressing need for faster organizational response, it does not make our pain go way.

It is always frustrating to have to learn to use a newly mandated computer office suite, after it took so long to master the old one. It is sometimes boring to sit through a weeklong quality seminar. And it is always annoying to have to play "phone-tag" five times before making actual contact. When we come right down to it, being forced to reschedule today's lunch hour can occasionally exhaust our current reservoir of self-adaptability! But all of these accommodations are the necessary minutiae of today's job-effective agent of change.

One does not ever learn self-adaptability to the point that it becomes unthinkingly automatic. Rather it is like decisions on sobriety. It comes one day and one turned-down drink at a time. And being homeostatic humans, we may fall off the self-adaptability wagon from time to time. Yet job-effective people distinguish themselves by making that decision to positively adapt most of the time.

Self-adaptability particularly manifests itself in the empowering quality of resourcefulness. Many a "wannabe" change agent becomes easily stymied by the lack of resources. Every enterprise, paradoxically, whether thriving or dying, seems to find itself perpetually short of manpower, budget, and time. So inaction, when it comes to effecting change, does not have to look far for an excuse. But a real change agent always has available to him or her, something far better than an excuse. It is the greatest resource of all—an unfailing sense of *resourcefulness*. A way to make it happen "in spite of...." It is well to remember that every successful start-up venture and every successful turn-around of a failing enterprise is more about resourcefulness than resources.

Agents of change are the surfboarders of this new-millennium commerce. They are perceptive enough to sense the next towering opportunity wave; eager enough to catch it; and agile enough to ride it. Characteristically, these game-changers are resilient enough to climb back on board each time they get "flipped."

Lastly, change agents especially understand the importance of changing themselves before attempting to change others, or the situations surrounding them. The popular book, "The Seven Habits of Highly Effective People"[10] expresses it this way: "Seek first to understand and then be understood."

Harry Truman Knew How to Self-Adapt.

There may be no better historic example of self-adaptability than that of President Harry S. Truman. His early life took many turns: farm boy, World War One artillery captain, Main Street haberdasher, and county "administrative" judge. Each earlier role in some unforeseen way seems to have prepared him for the next. He was a physically slight man, who had to learn to prod farm animals, give orders to battle-wise NCO's, calm fussing customers, and outfox Kansas City politicians. It did not come easy to Harry, whose boyhood inclinations leaned far more towards serious books, and a painful shyness.

"I've had a few setbacks in my life, but I never gave up," was how Truman later spoke of his ability to self-adapt. And so he went on to become a highly job-effective, if not attention grabbing, US Senator. This rare attribute combination would later suit the vain Roosevelt just fine in his wary choice of a Vice Presidential running mate.

With Roosevelt's death on April 12th, 1945, Truman became the non-elected leader of the free world. A stunned and doubting press openly questioned if he would be up to the task. But self-adapt did Truman! Within a few months of taking office he confidently met Churchill and Stalin on the world stage to re-map post war Europe. And weeks later, he was called upon to make one of the most momentous decisions of all times in the use of the atomic bomb.

Determined Russians blockading Berlin, an overly election confident Tom Dewey, the god-like General Mac Arthur, and the politically mighty rail and steel workers are but a few of those, who were to learn firsthand of Harry's extraordinary ability to self-adapt as the circumstances demanded.

Perhaps, Truman's greatest exercise in self-change was the day he left the White House, and quietly boarded the train at Union station to return, once again, with his beloved wife, Bess, to the quiet life of Independence, Missouri. Whether as world leader, or as small town, private citizen, he did both equally well. His was a "class act" in the difficult art of self-adaptability. [11]

****

Key Attributes #5 & #6 -Commitment & Follow-Up

Like energy and effort, the job-effective attributes of commitment and follow-up are an inseparable pair. So we need to consider them together. One tends to re-enforce the other. It is often intriguing to observe how much energy and effort we are willing to expend in attaining some desired goal or beneficial change, only to let it slip through our hands once we have begun to achieve it. The American near-religion of dieting is a good example. Every day, tens of millions of people endure a medium to long-term stay in a culinary hell trying to lose twenty or more pounds. Sooner or later their bathroom scale tells of a battle won, and Nirvana achieved. They are now the figure shapes that they were always meant to be. But alas, wait just six months! The new "petite-sized" wardrobe now hides in the back of the closet, and that long planned beach vacation seems like an awful idea.

As much as we need energy and effort to effect a beneficial change, so much the more do we need a strong sense of commitment to establish a foundation for change. Commitment is what sees us safely through all the doubting curves and uphill climbs that meaningful change often encounters. For real change has the propensity to become unglued as time passes. We think of Commitment as that dedicated determination, fueled by belief that we feel in our hearts to a cause or task.

The need is no less for a sense of follow-up to sustain that unfolding change until the last brick is firmly cemented in place. Just as initiative is vision expressed in action, so too, with follow-up. Follow-up is our sense of commitment translated into extended action. It's that continuing, seat-of-the-pants effort to see a job through long after those initial stirrings cease that got us moving towards a goal in the first place. As such up "follow-up" is most often seen walking around; not reading reports behind the desk.

Systematic follow-up is also vital in spreading our own feeling of commitment to others, who are not quite on-board yet with a recently initiated change. In any organization there will always be the doubters who view every change as the company's flavor-of-the-month selection, and be inclined to adopt a "this-too-will-pass" approach. More troublesome, a few may even actively oppose the change in the form of an orchestrated but hidden resistance. Unspoken resistance is perhaps the greatest challenge encountered in implementing a beneficial change. But it can be overcome by dedicated follow-up on the part of the change agent. A thorough job in the gathering and evaluating phases of the work process will do much to give the agent the confidence needed to overcome these resistance hurdles during the implementation stage.

Product Quality: The Supreme Test Of Commitment And Follow-up.

Perhaps, there are no better examples of the distinct but related roles that commitment and follow-up play in creating beneficial change than the quality crisis common to most businesses. Quality improvement is the eternal diet struggle of the working world. Today, our business and professional worlds routinely subscribe to programs such as "Total Customer Satisfaction, "Total Quality Management," "Six-Sigma," and "Zero Defects." They are all long bumpy roads to the same destination; trouble-free products not only delivered to the customer but just as importantly from the cost-competitive standpoint, produced in a trouble-free way.

As has been mentioned previously, experts estimate that the total organizational costs associated with poor quality averages somewhere between twenty and thirty percent of every sales dollar. So, on the positive side, there is not a surer way for a company to improve its fortunes than to bring its quality performance as near to zero-defects as is humanly possible. General Electric, by way of example, is a corporation widely admired for the ability to consistently provide their shareholders with attractive financial returns. GE attributes much of their recent success to their broad and rigorous adoption of the Six Sigma program. This is a total quality effort that sets a lofty goal of keeping employee mistakes or product faults to the statistically vanishing level of several parts per million!

On the negative side of the ledger, nothing is so corrosive to good customer relationships than product quality levels that are either declining, or show no long-term trend of improvement.

Because of these factors, there are few executives, these days, who do not with some regularity act like absolute "bears" when it comes to the subject of quality. They angrily write about the need for improvement in company publications; they constantly harp on it at employee get togethers; they threaten managerial bonuses; and they respond quickly and personally to every customer complaint. There can be little doubt of their commitment.

But poor quality, like a chronic infection, does not yield easily. It takes mega-doses of follow-up. For "unquality" is a disease with many symptoms, not just one. There are mistaken quantities, marginal designs, lost shipments, cosmetic defects, unclear assembly instructions etc., etc.

For the first few weeks of any quality improvement campaign the determined executives attend every meeting, chanting the mantra, "We are going to solve this quality issue once and for all." Unfortunately, the causes of poor quality are usually rooted in a multitude of tiny, arcane, and time-consuming details. They are rarely the stuff executives are particularly comfortable dealing with, nor are they always in line with their personal expertise. So, it is not long before the bored and frustrated executive is skipping the meetings, or designating a subordinate to "act for him." Soon, the rest of the Quality Improvement team is postponing, skipping, and delegating. Follow-up goes limp, and so goes the QI program, until six months later, when a new crisis brings about another blistering, "once-and-for-all-we-are-going-to-solve" meeting.

The reality is that words like time-consuming, frustrating, detail-laden, and boring really do characterize follow-up. As such, follow-up is probably the first attribute, to sneak out of our sixpack of work ethics. So, if we are to be job-effective change agents, we will constantly have to "follow-up" on our follow-up!

Putting The Six Work Ethic Factors to Work.

Now that we have developed a common understanding of the six traits that go to make up the change agent's work ethic, we can begin to see how they fit in with the three-stage work process of gathering, evaluating and implementing. Certainly, energy and effort are required throughout the entire process, but especially once a project is launched and the initial rushes of enthusiasm and adrenaline start to evaporate.

Self-adaptability is continually demanded in big and small doses throughout the entire work process. It is the hallmark of the work ethic in today's ever-changing world. Credibility and commitment are also work ethic traits that have to be at the ready from start to finish. Nothing will derail a program quicker than a midpoint lapse of personal credibility, or a wavering commitment on the part of the initiator. Initiative on the other hand is obviously an upfront quality that leads the charge of the beneficial change march, while follow-up is what is needed to take care of the back-end stragglers.

Discussion Problems.

1. Which of the six attributes of the work ethic do you feel you possess to the greatest degree? Which one is in need of the most development?
2. Pick three individuals you consider to be outstanding workers in your organization. On the basis of one to five, how would they score in each attribute of the sixpack?
3. What are the three predominant working styles in your organization? Do they add up to a culture?
4. You have just made a detailed presentation to your management on a significant cost savings proposal that you have developed. Everyone is very enthusiastic and gives you an immediate "go-ahead." In fact, the company president invites you to lunch, where he compliments you for your initiative and thoroughness. A few days later, in reviewing your supporting data, you find that you have made a miscalculation. You now estimate the annual cost savings will be more like $300,000 than $500,000. What should you do?

5. You work in the Production department. Recently, your department has been having difficulty getting work out due to software troubles with one of the new computerized processing machines that you recently installed. You have discussed this problem a number of times with your boss. Yesterday afternoon a major customer called your Vice President to complain about constantly late product shipments. The VP calls a meeting to discuss the customer complaint with you and your boss. At the meeting your boss never mentions the software problems with the new processing machine. Instead, he strongly implies that the cause of the late shipments lies with constantly delayed production releases from the Engineering Department. After listening to your boss, the VP turns to you and asks, "Do you have anything to add Joan?" How would you answer?

6. You have built a reputation over many years for being the hardest and most dedicated worker in your department. Recently, in a routine physical, your doctor picks up signs of some significant cardiac problems. He strongly advises you to reduce your work activities "thirty to forty percent." What if anything will you tell them at work?

7. Your boss has already asked you twice this summer to delay your vacation because of difficulties in meeting an important project deadline. You agreed. Now he comes to you for a third time, just one week before your children must start the new school year. How will you handle this request?

Chapter 5–Teaming

No (Working) Man Is An Island.

In the previous chapters there was a tacit focus on our individual performances in the quest for job-effectiveness. But the reality of the working world is that there are few customer-desired beneficial changes of any consequence that are successfully implemented without the coordinated efforts of a number of people. Introduction of virtually any commercial product to the marketplace will routinely require teams of engineers to develop it, manufacturing experts to produce it, and marketing people to sell it. Supporting them will be a quality staff to test the product, accountants to price it, a shipping group to deliver it, and a customer service team to take care of the product in the field.

Still, these are only the rudiments of the needed team to make a product a success. To cite just a few more, lawyers will be called in to make sure that the product complies with all governmental laws and regulations, and packaging engineers will be employed to make sure the product can be delivered to the customer without damage. After that, advertising experts will be needed to tell the product story to potential customers, and display experts will be called upon to make sure that the product offering has shelf appeal on the sales floor.

Even such a seemingly solo activity as writing a book, requires the review skills of editors and proofreaders, the artistry of a cover designer, and all the comprehensive printing, and marketing resources of the publisher and book handlers, if the publication is to achieve any measure of success. Indeed, perhaps fifty to a hundred people will be actively involved in applying their specialized, professional skills in order to put a book in customer's hands.

The vast majority of us find ourselves trained in fairly specialized skills; working for organizations that range in size from a dozen to hundreds of thousands of people; and grouped into specific functional departments. And while the functional departments provide us with an organizational home base, we are called upon to accomplish our basic work tasks not as individuals, but often much more job-effectively as members of a *team.* So, in order to be job-effective agents of change, we are going to have to reflect a bit on what it means to be part of a work team.

The Team Dynamic.

From the fundamental point of view of the overall *work process*, there is no real difference in a team approach from that of an individual effort. The team is formed to accomplish one or more customer-valued beneficial changes. Once the identity of the customer is established, and the mission to be achieved have been accepted by the team, the same three steps are sequentially followed. We gather the relevant facts, evaluate the alternatives, and then implement the most favorable choice.

What is quite different, of course, is the interactive dynamics that are brought about by the diversity of skills, personalities, and work styles. The team approach has its obvious pluses and minuses. On the plus side of the balance sheet, teams properly organized, properly motivated, and with the right panoply of skills can attack complex problems with great job-effectiveness in terms of speed and thoroughness. On the other side of the ledger, poorly led or poorly structured teams are extremely vulnerable to the down sides of those same human interactions. These advantages and risks of teaming rapidly compound the bigger or more complex the desired change, and the larger and more diverse the team. So effectively organizing the team for concerted action becomes critical.

Let's Listen to Some Music.

In order to develop an understanding of the basics of the team approach, let us imagine an assemblage of the world's most accomplished concert musicians on one stage with a renowned conductor at the podium. Now, suppose at the exact moment that the conductor signaled with his baton, each musician began to play as beautifully and soulfully as he or she could. But contrary to plan, each began playing a composition of their individual choosing. Needless to say the results would be disastrous, and the audience left to wonder. Next, suppose that after some baton throwing, the conductor secured the agreement of each musician to play the particular symphony that *he* had planned for that evening. As they started again, however, the strings chose to play the first movement, the horns launched into the second, while the percussion section led off with the third. Again, the result would be an unmitigated disaster, and some of the audience might even be expected to boo. Now, assume after some furious foot-stomping and head banging that the maestro managed to terrorize the orchestra into still a third attempt to play the same piece, and the same movement together. But this time the musicians were so intimidated that their timing was wildly off, the violin section began to rush, the horns seemed unable to keep up, and the drums turned sullen. On this last attempt, the symphony might at least be recognizable, but hardly satisfying.

Orchestras provide us with an excellent example of the concepts underlying effective teaming:

1. There must be a designated and competent leader to conduct the orchestra. A team must also have a strong leader.
2. There must be skilled musicians with diverse instruments to follow that lead. In the same way, work teams need players with a diversity of skills.
3. The orchestra needs to have a clear, up-front agreement about what particular composition will be played. To put it in our job-effectiveness terms, the team must first understand what specific customer–valued, beneficial change is to be achieved.
4. Just as there is a structural order of movements in musical compositions, so too, there is a natural and sequential order of gathering, evaluating and implementing change in the process of work. Moreover, these three steps must be paced by a reasonable and harmonious simultaneity of effort by each team member.

There is one final lesson that can be gleaned from this orchestral analogy —even great musicians meld into a world-class orchestra only through practice, practice, and more practice. It is the same, in the work-world! Great "can-do" teams have a track record of working together.

Problem Based Learning: An Ideal Tool For Teams.

One of the most effective ways that has been found to capitalize on the strengths of the team approach is known as Problem Based Learning. PBL has been employed for nearly forty years to train medical students in the clinical diagnosis and treatment of patients.[12] Needless to say, the complexities of the human body and the variability of a patient's symptoms frequently present a daunting challenge to the student-doctor. Yet, a well thought out treatment plan based on a sound diagnosis is something that he or she must learn to do efficiently and accurately.

It has been found that the best way this skill can be acquired is for the students to work in collaborative teams. Typically a team of four to six persons is used for each case presented. The teams pursue the following steps in arriving at a diagnosis:

1. The patient's symptoms, past history, and laboratory findings are thoroughly discussed by the group.
2. The team members generate multiple hypotheses as to what might be the underlying causes of a particular illness.
3. "Learning issues" that present diagnostic stumbling blocks for the group are identified, and assigned to individual team members to be immediately researched.
4. Information gathered on the assigned learning issues is shared as soon as possible with the other team members.
5. Lastly, by systematically evaluating each suggested hypothesis, the team reaches a group consensus of the most probable diagnosis.

Once a probable diagnosis has been established, the same process of hypothesis generation, resolution of identified learning issues, and group consensus is developed regarding an appropriate treatment plan.

Problem Based Learning is the work process of gathering, evaluating, and implementing change that is performed on a team basis. It is founded on the common sense idea that multiple heads are generally better than one in solving a complicated problem. Thus, properly applied, PBL offers both speed and completeness in complex problem solving.

Diagnosis and Treatment in The World Of Enterprise.

The PBL method is now finding its way into the business world as the team philosophy increasingly gains ground. Like the clinical situation, most enterprise problems presented for team resolution have a "diagnostic" aspect as well as a "treatment" aspect. Almost always, it is necessary for the team to first precisely define the problem that will be solved. Thus, the boss might tell us, "to find out why our shipping costs have recently skyrocketed," or that "our product quality efforts seem to be slipping." Before we can devise an effective solution, we must translate the manager's vaguely expressed complaints into a set of facts that can be addressed. Understanding whether the mailroom team has become lazy, or is simply swamped trying to handle all the employees' Christmas cards and personal packages, obviously will lead to two very different treatments. Unlike, MBA classes, real world problems that are presented to teams are seldom accompanied by a thoroughly documented case study!

There are two other advantages to the PBL methodology that recommend its use in the business problem solving setting: First, the consensus discussions tend to build high levels of understanding, involvement, and commitment among the entire team. Second, the assignment of individualized learning issues is an efficient way of gathering all the disparate pieces of information that complex problem solving demands.

Lead, Follow, Or Get Out Of The Way!

In Chapter 2 we talked about a poster sign that advised us of the three-choice decision we must continually make in today's fast moving environment of enterprise. Well, here it is again! It is the first law of effective teaming.

LEAD!!

FOLLOW!..OR,

GET OUT OF THE WAY!

Figure 5.1. The First Law of Teaming.

A team of course, can be as small as two people assembled to accomplish some ad-hoc, afternoon task, or as large as a multimillion man army charged with saving the republic. No matter what, those three choices neatly sum up ninety-five percent of what the dynamics of teaming is all about! Someone has to be willing to lead the team, some others have to be willing to follow, and the rest of us, who are not directly involved, have to have the good sense to get out of the way. So, let's examine those choices in some detail.

Who Should Be the Leader?

In the past the question of who should be the designated leader of a team rarely arose. The boss predictably appointed either himself, or the same senior person—his "right hand man"—to the leadership role. But the new era of accelerating global competition, technical complexity, fast-changing opportunities, and new daily challenges, demands an ever-changing panorama of leadership skills. These needed skills are rarely found in a single individual. Experience in its repetitious form of "been-there-done-that," goes only so far in effectively dealing with any brand new situation. So there is a need for the leadership mantle to be shared by a number of people as diverse opportunities arise.

How then should the choice of a leader in a particular situation be made? The starting criteria seem fairly obvious. The chosen leader should:

1. Have a reputation for being a job-effective agent of change.
2. Be willing to serve in a leadership role.
3. Realistically have the required time to devote to the project.
4. Be respected by, and respectful of, the other team members.
5. Have an in-depth understanding of the dominant issues that determine the outcome of the project.

This understanding of the leader may sometimes require a general management capability for large projects where organizing, budgeting and planning skills are critical for the leadership role. At other times it may be a highly specialized technical expertise. For example, when a small team investigates the therapeutic value of a new drug.

Exercising Leadership.

Once the leader has been selected, he or she will then:

1. Pick, or at least have a consulting role in the selection of the other team members.
2. Clarify and secure the agreement of the whole team as to who is the customer, and what beneficial change is being sought.
3. Organize the team members into roles that best guarantee a successful outcome.
4. Mutually define with each team member his or her role, specific tasks, and expected completion dates.

5. Set the overall timetable for the three-phase work process of gathering, evaluating and implementing the desired outcome.
6. Monitor and report the progress as the team executes the tasks required to meet the end goal.
7. Make mid-course corrections as needed.

The "Make-It-Happen" Roles of the Followers.

In job-effective teaming a follower is neither a "gopher," nor just another pair of hands. Rather, he or she is seen as having a key and unique skill required in the chain of events necessary to implement a beneficial change. As such followers can often be more senior or more skilled in one or more ways than the leader. Depending on the need, a follower may be involved in either one or all three phases of the entire work process. A job-effective follower:

1. Develops at the outset of the project a detailed understanding of the overall team goals and his or her particular role.
2. Performs the assigned tasks in a skillful, complete, and timely fashion.
3. Loyally accepts the consensus decisions of the entire team, after having been given an opportunity to express his or her personal position.
4. Makes every effort to work out other current job responsibilities so that the team time schedule can be maintained.
5. Keeps the team leader informed of progress in carrying out the assigned tasks.

Unlike the leader, who must frequently deal with the sometimes aggravating matters of scheduling, budgeting, personnel concerns, and organizational reporting, the team followers can expect to spend the bulk of their time exercising and honing their individual professional skill sets. Thus, following often has its own built-in set of rewards.

The Rare Choice: Getting Out of the Way.

Needless to say, all of us not selected to work on a particular team assignment have a responsibility at a very minimum, to do nothing to impede the progress of the team. On the contrary, job-effective employees help another team's progress whenever, and as best they can from the sidelines. Even when they strongly disagree with another team's assigned goals they recognize that they might not have the "whole story." In any event, they also understand that pebble-throwing only invites rock-sized paybacks.

But what if a person finds himself assigned to a team whose goals he or she cannot honestly support, or for which they feel totally unqualified? Here, the appropriate thing for this team member is to first discuss with the leader his or her concerns, to see if they can be resolved. If they cannot, the team member should ask for a different assignment, rather than turn-in a half-hearted or marginal performance. Of course, this third option should be exercised rarely, and only after having walked the extra mile before coming to this decision. Sitting it out, too often, can quickly earn a worker a prima donna status, and perhaps even an employer decision that his or her services can be dispensed with entirely.

Some Issues Of Leadership.

As we have already seen, deciding to be a follower on the team is an easy choice for us; most likely we will have been asked to join the team because of our reputation for doing some particular activity especially well. Thus it becomes an opportunity to enjoy job-satisfaction as much as it is to demonstrate job-effectiveness. And a decision not to participate on a team ought to be a very rare option. The real challenge is the decision to accept the team leadership role when offered. It raises four questions:

1. How often should I be selected as leader?
2. What is my level of commitment?
3. What real power do I have?
4. How do I deal with difficult people?

Each of us must ask these questions of ourselves if we are going to be truly job-effective change agents. The first two of these issues will be covered in the remainder of this chapter. The last two will be the entire subject of the next chapter.

How Often Should I Expect to Be the Selected Leader?

The answer to this question is fairly easy; some of the times, but certainly, not all the time! A good manager selects team leaders depending on the scope of the task, and the need to fulfill already existing commitments. Sometimes, she will select a highly senior person based on the complexity, or the urgency, of the job to be done. At other times, she will see a good opportunity for a less experienced person to develop leadership skills. The point is that there are a variety of tasks, which need to be accomplished in the typical organization, and the opportunity for some leadership assignments should fall to everyone over a reasonable time. If an individual is never chosen for a leadership assignment it may well be a signal that his actual or perceived job-effectiveness is not what it should be. Whatever the reason, the problem needs to be cleared-up by some honest discussions with the appropriate supervisor.

On the other hand, it is impossible for any one individual to have the time and skills to effectively lead more than one or two sizable projects at any given time. If an individual always finds himself taking on the leadership position, he is either totally surrounded by incompetents, or held prisoner by his

own ego. Most likely it's the latter. In any event, neither case bodes well for his long-term career. Instead of doing a credible job on a few key assignments, he will simply end up doing a half-baked job on a half -dozen.
Once having accepted the leadership mantle it is important that the leader continually remind himself that it his job to spend the bulk of his time leading the team. That means continually keeping the road ahead clear so that the progress of the team does not come to a halt.

The Need for Committed Leadership.

The writer once worked on a large team project effort where the leadership was not very good. The leader, who always seemed visibly annoyed, rushed through the weekly progress review meetings, if he held them at all. It was obvious he was much more interested in the intricacies of his

THE SIX STAGES OF A PROJECT.

1. WILD ENTHUSIASM.
2. GROWING DISILLUSIONMENT.
3. PANIC.
4. SEARCH FOR THE GUILTY.
5. PUNISHMENT OF THE INNOCENT.
6. REWARDS AND HONORS FOR THE NON-PARTICPANTS.

Figure 5.2 The Story Board Of A Poorly Led Team.

engineering specialty than in guiding a team effort. So everybody was left, more or less, to follow their own agenda.

On our team was a senior technician by the name of Jerry. He was a quiet man, who rarely engaged in anything other than straight technical discussions. But he had an 8 ½ inch by 11.0 inch Xeroxed chart hung obscurely on the wall by his desk that was entitled, "The Six Phases Of A Project." It is reproduced in figure 5.2.

Jerry had a little magnetic arrow, which he moved from time to time to the appropriate phase, as he perceived the downhill slide of the program. Amusingly, yet sadly, Jerry always seemed to have it about right! Without sustained and dedicated leadership any team effort is likely to follow the story board outlined in figure 5.2. Team leadership is indeed a serious responsibility!

It is always tempting for the leader, especially one with a technical background, to absorb himself in some particular team task that happens to strike his personal interest. Here is a particular example: A fairly senior manager, whose mission was to reduce material procurement costs among several divisions, spent weeks "inventing" his own complex, fourteen-digit coding system for part numbers. He took on this complicated and detail-oriented task despite just having appointed a four-man task force for that very purpose! Not surprisingly, it was never implemented by the team, despite his daily badgering as to its unsurpassed excellence. Instead his Materials Control masterpiece suffered the well-known organizational fate known as "slow death by a thousand small cuts." Needless to say, the teams overriding objective of reducing material costs fared little better.

How A Great Leader Defines Today's Leaders.

Jack Welch, CEO of GE, and legendary for his own leadership skills, offers this vision of the ideal GE employee-leader of the future:

"We must raise, again, the bar of quality as it applies to ourselves. The reality is, we simply can't afford to field anything but teams of 'A' players. What is an 'A'? At the leadership level an 'A' is a man or woman with a vision, and the ability to articulate that vision to the team so vividly and powerfully that it also becomes their vision. An 'A' leader has enormous personal energy...and the ability to energize others. An 'A' leader has "edge," the instinct and courage to make the tough calls. As we go forward, there will be nothing but 'A's' in every leadership position in this company. They will be the best in the world, and they will act to field teams consisting of nothing but 'A' players"[13]

Discussion Problems.

1. You have just been appointed the leader of a key product development program. Jim comes to you, and urges you to give him the responsibility for the engineering design. In three previous design efforts Jim did well with the most recent one, OK on the second, and poorly on the third. How will you decide? Explain why.

2. Your team is midway through a yearlong effort to consolidate two operations. Mary has done an excellent job handling all the financial analysis relating to the consolidation. Yesterday she asked you to remove her from the team immediately because of a "personal conflict." She refuses to elaborate. What do you do?

3. Mike has recently been promoted to Division Controller. You replaced him as Supervisor of Accounts Payable, a position Mike held for five years. After working with Mike on several team efforts during the past few months, you realize he is continuing to do all the payable portions of the job himself. Although you have the formal responsibility for this work, you feel rather useless as a team member. How would you be inclined to resolve this problem?

4. The following factors are often cited as being important in determining the success or failure of a team effort. Based on your opinion, rate each of these factors on a "1 to 5" scale:
   a) Leadership abilities of the team leader.
   b) Bonding of the team.
   c) Clear mission and goals.
   d) Project visibility to the senior management.
   e) Demonstrated support of the customer.
   f) Adequate budget resources.
   g) Promises of recognition and rewards upon success.
   h) Group consensus on how the work effort will proceed.
   i) Co-location of the team.

5. Your boss asks you to take over an existing project effort that has not been going well. He informs you that the project is now four months late, and that spending is already twice what was anticipated. You also learn that the original team leader suddenly quit the company after a barrage of complaints from his teammates. Outline an agenda that you intend to cover at your first meeting with the team.

Chapter 6–The Company Zoo

Leadership Without Power.

As we have already noted in the previous chapter, one of the good things about the new globally competitive world of business is the need for many team leaders to deal with diverse, complex, and fast changing issues. This is quite a change from having a few, crusty, autocratic managers who "ran everything by the book" as in the 1970's. But as the need for many leaders has proliferated, their authority to make things happen in the team environment has become increasingly vague. Management textbooks try to put the best face on this leadership-without-defined-power situation by using the term "influence management." This euphemism not withstanding, the concept of accountability without authority is not all that reassuring. Just ask anyone who has had the unfortunate weekend experience of "baby sitting" for somebody else's overly rambunctious teenagers!

The fortunate reality of the work environment is that we are likely to encounter this kind of leadership authority challenge from only a small number of individuals. The vast majority of our teammates want to do a good job, and keep their own egos in check. They are willing to follow the leadership of any competent individual who treats the team players with respect.

Pareto's 90/10 Rule.

To put this whole issue of being a team leader, as opposed to a hire-and-fire boss in perspective, it might be useful to reflect on what is known as Pareto's law. Pareto was a late nineteenth century economist. His socially oriented research led him to the observation that 90 % of the crimes committed in any given region could be attributed to about 10 % of the population. In general it has been found that lots of undesirable things follow Pareto's 90/10 rule, and the workplace is no exception. For example, 90% of the lateness for work will be attributable to about 10% of the employees. And typically, 10% of a company's product lines will cause 90% of the quality problems.

More to the point under discussion, it seems that at any given time, the job performance of up to ten percent of an organization's team players will fall below a minimum acceptable standard. And on occasion there may even be some outright mischief makers on board despite the determination of every organization to hire responsible, job-effective workers.

So if we happen to be the leader, but not the real hire- and-fire boss, what can we do about that one in ten team member, who is going to cause us some headaches one way or another? Well, as a very first step we can take great comfort in the good ninety percent that generally make-up our teams. For personal and group reasons they want the team to succeed. And although they might not always speak out directly, they are sensitive to and intolerant of anyone either not pulling their full weight, or who is intent on de-railing the success of the project. In fact, there is a certain tribal discipline, which comes about with the formation of a committed team. It is quite effective in enforcing good behavior among those who might otherwise be inclined to rock the boat.

Second, it is important to keep in mind that the troublesome ten percent are not unique to our team or our leadership. Misfits are just part of the landscape. Sometimes for far longer than anybody can understand why, especially in today's "lean and mean" environment. Dealing with people whose job-effectiveness is not up to par goes with the leadership territory.

Third, there is great advantage, whether team leader or not, in having some pre-understanding of the types of individuals who create difficulties for the functioning of teams. It is the old saying of, "It being far better to deal with a devil that you have encountered before ..."

In the following pages, eight different "species" of problem teammates will be described. In any large organization they comprise a kind of virtual company zoo. Their managers keep them hidden and caged-up as much as possible, while they build a case for dismissal, scheme of arranging lateral transfers, or fantasize that these troublemakers might actually quit. It will be surprising if you have not met up with at least some of these creatures before as we walk past the various exhibits!

Exhibit #1- Mr. R.F. Aim.

One of the key concepts of working on a team basis is maintaining a harmonious pace as we go through the work process of gathering, evaluating and activating. It is not an easy task! Chances are, on any large team, you will encounter two classic types of individuals who can drive you crazy when it comes to maintaining an effective pace.

The first of these pace-upsetting creatures is Mr. Ready Fire Aim. R. F. Aim is an action-oriented kind of fellow, who has little patience with the gathering and evaluation phases of the beneficial change process. If the goal is to take the hill from the enemy, he will not waste time reconnoitering whether an approach from the north is better than the south, or how many machine gun nests, walled-cliffs, and barb-wired barricades just might stand in the way. In fact Aim, doesn't particularly care if taking the hill is a worthwhile objective. He just wants to get on with a John Wayne style frontal attack. There is something fundamentally American, macho, and even glorious about the ACTION phase of the change process. After all, how many movies have we seen where the Duke says, "I really would like to sit down with you guys for a couple of days to plan this whole thing out"? No way, we have to save the girl, hang the thief, or take the hill—PRONTO! Aim's approach is exactly the same, "Let the wimps gather and evaluate, later when we have the time!"

At his funeral Aim would love to hear himself remembered as "results-oriented." Of course, Mr. Ready Fire often quickly gets to the top of the hill only to find that it is the wrong hill. Never mind though, without pause or apology he runs back down and charges up the next one in sight.

This is not to say that Mr. Aim is all bad! On a major long-term development effort his premature and frequent forays can be a real headache. On the other hand, situations arise everyday when an organization teeters on disaster—for example, a critical machine suddenly fails on a high volume assembly line. However desirable it might be in theory, there is not a lot of time to sit around and pontificate on what to do next. There is a need to cut to the chase with a rapid series of "Try this...!" Aim can usually be counted on to get things up and running after two or three furious assaults on the problem. So, more often than not, he is well worth the piles of scrap, the shouting matches, and bruised egos that come along with his help. Nevertheless, once the crisis has subsided, the team leader often finds himself busily chasing Mr. Aim around in an effort to coax him back into his cage.

Exhibit #2- Mr. G. R. Squared.

The polar opposite of Ready-Fire-Aim is Mister Get Ready Squared. Unlike R.F.Aim, Old G.R. loves being in a cage, where he can spend the rest of his working life getting ready to get ready. This particular species has decided early in his career to make a specialty of the gathering phase of the work process.

He is not difficult to spot. He tends to be a serious fellow, definitely more intelligent than smart; spends endless hours working hard; and considers himself "thorough," "careful," and above all, "prudent." His desk is piled high with arcane reference materials, and his notepad is full of self-reminders of places to visit, people to talk to, and the latest statistical reports that must be read. He is willing to talk interminably about the details of his assignment, but there are some words that will never cross his lips like: "I'm finished," "We could meet now," or "Let's go ahead and do it." Occasionally, under extreme group pressure he ventures into the realm of the evaluation phase, but then only tentatively. "Perhaps, we are starting to get a sense that......" is about as far as his neck reaches out! After which, of course, comes his standard admonition on the need for more data, more time, and naturally more funding.

G. R. Squared puts one in mind of that certain kind of driver who goes down the center lane of a crowded and fast moving expressway at about thirty miles an hour less than everybody else. His left turn signal is permanently locked-on, and all the while he is sanctimoniously clucking away at the damn fools passing him on either side. You risk a heart attack if you get stuck behind him and a major fender-bender if you dare to pass!

And so it is with G. R. Squared in the team setting. Everyone else is aggravated by the lack of real progress, and tries to figure out how to best get around him. If you are the team leader, you have a real challenge on your hands with Mr. Squared! You cannot change his work style because he is so self-righteous; you cannot get him fired because of his long standing reputation for working hard; and you cannot get him transferred to another department because of his equally long reputation for never getting anything done. The only thing to do is drive around him.

Exhibit # 3- Mr. MASEF.

This next fellow to be described has a personal problem, which often translates into a performance issue as a team player. Fortunately, the problem is one that is amenable to what the psychiatrists like to call the "talking cure." And it might well be worth the time investment it takes of the leader to effect the cure, because this kind of individual often can become a very effective team member, once a deeply felt, but unarticulated problem is taken care of. Let's call this particular individual Mr. MASEF, which we will use as an acronym for "mad-about-something-easily- fixed."

To illustrate the MASEF syndrome, take the real-life case of an engineer, who we will call Tom. Tom MASEF, was a middle-aged bachelor. Unlike many engineers of a similar vintage, he always backed up his designs with a rigorous mathematical analysis, instead of relying on a few, quick rules-of-thumb which designers tend to pick-up with years of experience. There are times when this kind of formal analysis is absolutely essential, and so Tom was well respected by both the management and his professional associates.

In the first ten years Tom was with the firm, he seemed to be very happy and satisfied. But for no obvious reason Tom suddenly started to become very critical of just about everything at work; the management, the kind of projects being worked on, the food in the cafeteria, and even how the last company picnic was run. He also started to wear a baseball cap everyday in the office, which was particularly strange for a man who fastidiously favored conservatively cut, three-piece suits. It was not long before Tom augmented his wide-ranging criticisms with some scarcely concealed threats to leave the company. And as his attacks on the management became more and more strident, some of the executives were beginning to think it might not be such a bad idea if he would leave.

Well, as you might expect, it was not long before Tom ended up in his supervisor's office for the kind of heart to heart talk that this kind of situation demands. In fact, there were three such hour-long meetings over the next couple weeks where Tom repeated in a rambling and unconvincing fashion all the things that were wrong with the company. George, his boss, calmly tried to offer counter arguments that would persuade Tom that he was indeed mistaken. The third meeting was especially contentious, and as it was about to end, Tom let go with "this management treats us engineers like crap!"

"Listen to me Tom," George said in exasperation, "I'm not going to say everything around here is perfect. But the fact is that in the last six months this company has spent a fortune completely re-doing the engineering offices so we could have an attractive and functional place to work. Why, they have spent over a quarter-million dollars just putting in new ceiling lighting alone."

"Oh Yeah!!" Tom shouted back, flinging off his Sox cap. "And just look how that damned new florescent lighting of yours is bleaching out my thousand dollar hair piece!"

That very next morning, the lights directly over Tom's work area were changed back to the old lower-intensity tubes. By noon, Tom had taken off his baseball cap; replaced his recent scowl with a pleasant smile; and performed his much-valued engineering analyses happily ever after!

Whenever we encounter an effective team member who suddenly goes sour, and has nothing to offer but a litany of wild, unrelated complaints, the talking cure is certainly worth a try. It is surprising what unexpected things can become sore spots in the workplace. It is just as surprising how easily they can often be fixed by listening, listening, and listening.

Exhibit #4 - The Industrious Incompetent.

In Arthur Miller's classic play, "Death of a Salesman," there is the tragic figure of Willie Lohman. Described as "somewhat past sixty," Willie's entire business career has been at best mediocre. Half admitting, and half denying this to himself, and on the verge of being fired, he struggles anew each day with soaring, yet half-baked, plans to reverse the final outcome.

The Willie that you will meet in your teaming efforts might be twenty years younger than Lohman, but other than that, he is very much the same. He takes his job very seriously; works hard at it; and often has many years of service with the company. All in all, he is very likable. Unlike G.R. Squared, Willie is not afraid to tackle any phase of the work process. And unlike Ready-Fire-Aim, he spends the time planning, although often unrealistically, what he is going to do. It just seems that he never does a job right, and somebody else on the team has to cover for him. He feels awful when he screws-up, and re-doubles his efforts as a way of making amends.

In the old, life-long employment days, Willie was the prime candidate for a yearly inter-departmental transfer. Now, in the current lean-and-mean environment he ends up getting laid-off after a number of reprieves. Everybody feels real bad for Willie when it finally happens. In the meantime, the team leader will find himself spending much time trying to figure out the right assignments for Willie.

Enterprise: An Unmatched Opportunity For Heroes.

The story of the hero, living or dead, real or imagined, captivates all of us from early childhood to old age. So much so that the seeds of heroism are planted deep within us, just waiting for the opportunity to flower in myriad ways. There is an intriguing and profound book entitled, "The Hero With A Thousand Faces." It was written nearly fifty years ago by Joseph Campbell, an expert in mythology.[14] In this volume, Campbell analyzes in great detail the underlying theme elements and structure common to every hero story. Briefly, the heroic adventure includes most, if not all, of the following elements:

1. The would-be hero is called to accomplish a great and dangerous task by either a supernatural being, or an important assemblage of people.
2. He accepts the call and challenge at great personal sacrifice.
3. He is assaulted or hindered by a number of evil and overwhelming forces while trying to accomplish the task.
4. He snaps victory from the jaws of defeat only after a long and exhausting struggle, sometimes with the help of a "shadowy" guide.
5. Upon his return, he receives the acclamation of a grateful multitude for his outstanding deeds.

Enterprise provides at once a continuously revolving stage, and all the necessary ingredients, for the heroic role. The long term stability and financial progress of a company is often threatened by fierce competition, hostile takeovers, or technological obsolescence. A series of managerial miscalculations on needed investments, or the market acceptance of products, may also bring the company rapidly to the brink of disaster. Thus, there is always the need for those rare, but genuine, organizational heroes. The Iacocca types, who stop the dollar hemorrhage and organizational panic, re-invigorate the product offerings, and restore confidence.

On a lesser, everyday scale, mini-heroes also exist in business enterprises, who quietly take-on hundreds of less grand, but taxing tasks that selflessly advance the organizational well-being. Getting to serve or lead a team with one or more of these dedicated individuals provides each team member with a wellspring of motivation.

But there is also a far less helpful variant of the company hero, which we will term the pseudo-hero. Pseudo-heroes are that interesting group of workers, who invariably manage to transform any company mission, or team assignment into a grandiose ego trip. Often they do this with a finesse that both irritates and amazes their teammates. At the same time, the team leader finds himself wondering how to get his arms around these slippery individuals—maybe even by the neck! Four types of pseudo-heroes will now be described in our continuing tour of the company zoo. In order of appearance they are:

1. The Great White Knight.
2. The Lone Ranger.
3. Robin Hood.
4. Darth Vader.

<u>Exhibit #5- The Great White Knight In Shining Armor.</u>

Of the five basic elements of the hero role, enumerated above, the two that drive the Great White Knight to action are the first and the last; an exalted call to undertake a grand task, and the final acclamation of a deed well done. Conspicuously absent are the middle elements of engaging in a great struggle. Strutting around the office like a peacock, he is an easy fellow to spot. As befitting a great white knight, he conveys worldly success by dressing exceedingly well, and often driving a flashy car.

He is the first to volunteer for an assignment, provided only that the request for help is made from someone he regards as "important." Otherwise forget it! Never mind if the request is small; in due time he will transform it into a grand adventure; a major epic in the history of the company.

White Knight is a very gregarious fellow, engaging any and all in conversations, which invariably turn to himself and his most recent accomplishments. Although he regales in discussions of wars won, White Knight hates entering into the dirty and lengthy battles of working out the task details. His self-chosen role is the final slaying of the grand dragon; not beating-off the hundreds of cats and dogs that stand in the way. So when the epic of the hero comes to the point of the exhausting and drawn-out struggle, our hero friend quickly delegates the assignment to whomever he happens to run across. He pleads that headquarters needs him in Europe over the next couple of weeks. Perhaps, even hinting ominously that no less than the company chairman has picked him to take on an even more vital, rush task.

"Would it be possible then to meet with him to understand better the six man weeks of required work efforts that have just been dumped in your lap," you ask. Great Knight reaches into his vest pocket and glances gravely at his planner and replies, "Doesn't look good Charlie... Maybe Sunday morning at eight, but I can't promise. Why don't you check with my secretary, Jean, late Saturday afternoon...... Oh God, it is four fifteen ... I'll never make it to the airport! Don't worry Charlie, I know you will come through for us. I trust you! Bye, Bye!"

But rest assured its not good bye to the program! Great White Knight will be back on stage at the successful conclusion of the project, accepting the management kudos for another job well done by you and the rest of your weary teammates.

Exhibit #6- The Lone Ranger.

In many ways the Lone Ranger type of pseudo-hero is the exact opposite of a Great Knight. His dress is modest to sloppy, and he makes no special effort to call attention to himself. He has no interest in trying to impress the other members of the team with his considerable knowledge, at least for the moment. Let us call our Lone Ranger archetype Lonnie. Lonnie doesn't say a word at the initial team-planning meeting, when the goals are agreed upon and the team assignments are handed out. But Lonnie's mind is going at warp speed. Though outwardly polite, he has already decided that everybody else on the team is not too bright, especially the team leader.

Now, Lone Ranger receives the heroic call from on high; an inner voice saying that it is all really up to him. He dutifully responds by mapping out in his own mind exactly when, and how, he will accomplish the desired beneficial change, all by himself.

Unlike the Great White Knight, there is no project detail that is below Lone Ranger's ken or dignity. As the weeks unfold he does not attend the team meetings. People wonder whether Lonnie is still on the team. But there are reports from others in the organization that he is working feverishly and furtively on some project, which sounds a lot like what the team is supposed to be doing. Lonnie's responses to the team leader's queries as to his doings are at best cryptic. So the leader makes team re-assignments to cover for his absence.

Weeks pass with the rest of the team working hard; progress is apparent; and it is beginning to look like the world may go on without Lonnie anyway. But faster than a speeding bullet, and one week before the team is due to make their final management presentation, Lone Ranger drops his own grand solution to the problem on everybody's desk, including the Vice President's.

All things considered it's a good plan, and it is presented in the most sophisticated PowerPoint® format. The VP responds to this totally unexpected initiative by sending Lonnie a congratulatory e-mail on a job well done, then salts the wounds by copying all the rest of the team members. Hurriedly, the enraged team meets to plan a counterattack strategy. From now on it looks like the Lone Ranger will really be lonely!

Exhibit #7- Robin Hood.

The seventh species in our company zoo is the Robin Hood. This pseudo-hero type is quite a bit different than the other two in that he fully identifies with, and works hard for the team. On any given day he is quite handy to have around, but often, he can be quite a problem over the long run.

Robin Hood knows every inch of the company forest. He spends most of his time roaming in other departments, and establishing friendships and "contacts." Unlike White Knight whose sole purpose is noisy self–aggrandizement, or Lone Ranger, who wants to quietly upstage everybody else, Robin Hood gets his jollies by breaking the rules, ignoring procedures, or otherwise subverting the company management in the pursuit of the team's mission.

He sees himself as the anti-establishment type of hero, who robs or otherwise emasculates the "do-nothing" management solely for the good of the company minions laboring down in the trenches. If the project team needs another computer, but it is not in the budget, just mention it to Robin. Mysteriously one will appear in the project office that very night. Does the team not want to waste lots of time walking a block and a half to the company designated area for smoke breaks? Just go see Robin. Within days, the team office will be equipped with ashtrays, an exhaust fan, window curtains, and door locks.

After a while, as a team leader you might really get to depend on Robin. But just remember, he will have vanished deep into the woods, when the manufacturing department launches an investigation as to how the computer they ordered, and paid for three months ago, ended up being delivered to your team office!

Exhibit #8- Darth Vader.

In the case of all our corporate zoo characters described thus far, the leadership advice has been pretty much to work with these individuals to the extent you can, and work around them when you can not. It is somewhat like learning to live with arthritis or a trick knee; we just decide to get on with life!

This next and last individual is a much more dangerous animal to have roaming around, and one that the team leader is going to have to deal with head-on, if the group mission is to have any chance of success. Let us name this fellow Darth Vader, for he has his own hidden and destructive agenda. Your team's mission failure is his secret goal.

Darth seems to arrive on the company doorstep from outer space. He has a very impressive resume that details numerous accomplishments with a large number of different organizations. Once on board, he quickly shows that he is highly skillful, and knows how to get things done. Although his operating style is very mechanistic and unfeeling, his aggressive efforts often succeed in creating an early, favorable impression with the management. As a consequence he often makes rapid initial jumps in the organization.

But there is a darker side to Darth: he has uncontainable feelings of superiority, which he can only seem to relieve by constantly belittling the efforts of everybody else. "I'm going to give you a fast ride on a downhill skateboard," is the kind of put-down boast Darth likes to unload on another teammate, with whose task approach he happens to disagree. If confronted about this kind of behavior, Darth, totally unmoved, replies that he, "Just tells it like it is—no bull"

While Darth prefers to think of himself as being "candid, frank, and logical" his coworkers see him as a "mean and crude s.o.b." Politically, Vader is very savvy and two-faced. He favors a divide and conquer strategy. He continually makes and breaks flimsy alliances with other team members, as happens to suit his purpose at the moment. As an independent schemer, he loves withholding critical information from the team until the damage is complete. He also creates team dissension by constantly offering divisive input.

Alas, the seeds of Darth's ultimate destruction lie within himself; regarding all his peers as stupid and incompetent, he soon becomes bored playing his little mind games with them. So, he looks for more worthy challenges, and invariably sets his sights on practicing his tricks on someone higher up in the organization. Sooner or later Vader meets his match and when his rapid disappearance from the scene is confirmed, there is great rejoicing throughout.

Although, Darth ultimately receives his deserved comeuppance, he can create utter destruction to a team effort in the meanwhile. So this is one instance where a "grin and bear it" strategy is not going to work. In this kind of situation the leader has to go to his or her management, armed with the facts and make the demand that "something has gotta change here."

Don't Venture Into The Cages!

There is one last thought we might consider while reviewing the various species who make up the company zoo, and the kind of behaviors that give you trouble in your roles either as team leader or team member. The truth is that none of us is totally immune from becoming one of the eight inhabitants of this menagerie. The thrill of being an action oriented guy like Ready-Fire-Aim, the self-assured procrastinator like GR Squared, or having the delusions of grandeur of the Great White Knight will tempt all of us more than once in our careers. And then there is always the lure of the self-satisfying rebelliousness of a Lone Ranger or a Robin Hood.

A little less easily, the right set of unfortunate life experiences is what often gives birth to the unspoken problems of Mr. MASEF, the tragedy of a Willie Lohman, or even an alien spirit like Darth Vader. So, it is worthwhile every once in a while to do a self-check on our own operating styles before somebody else in the organization decides it would be best if we were kept in a cage! If we begin to find ourselves more and more sitting alone at the lunch table, it is probably time to make that self- assessment.

Discussion Problems.

1. Tony has been part of your sales team for the last five years. You consider his performance to be somewhat marginal in that his yearly quota averages are down in the range of 80%. Recently, however, Tony has landed a big order with one of his customers that should put him at 125% of the goal for this year. Since getting this order you notice that Tony has been making it a habit of coming to work later and later each day. Finally, this morning when Tony arrived at 10:00 AM you felt compelled to confront him about his frequent lateness. Tony did not

take the criticism very well. In fact he said to you, "I thought we were getting paid to achieve results around here, not just punch a clock!" What would you have said in reply to Tony?

2. Offices in your company are traditionally shared by two people, unless they are designated as senior managers. Norm comes to you, and complains that he is unable to concentrate on his work, and that he is becoming increasingly "nervous." He blames this on his office mate, Joe. According to Norm, Joe is constantly on the phone arguing with his ex-wife. Norm points out that there is a completely vacant office down the corridor. You suspect that Norm, who has an extremely high opinion of himself, just wants to enhance his sense of self prestige with a private office. How should this be resolved?

3. Phil is one of four people assigned to you on a team that is preparing an important proposal with a very tight deadline. He comes to you early one afternoon quite distraught, and informs you that he has just learned that his grandmother has died. Phil asks if it would be OK to take a couple days off as he is too upset to work. You express your sympathy, and assure him that you and the rest of the team will do their best to cover for him. That same night you happen to attend the Blackhawks hockey game, and to your chagrin you see Phil there having a grand time. What will you say to Phil at the game? When he returns to work?

4. Sue is by far the best and most experienced designer on your five-person team. However, in team meetings she tends to monopolize all the discussions. She is especially quick to throw cold water on any design ideas different

than her own. After several months you notice that the three younger engineers seem completely turned-off. What do you do?

5. Al, more or less, sits back at the initial team meeting, when the objectives are discussed and the individual assignments are worked out. As a member of the team, you leave the meeting believing it is a pretty good project. In fact, you look forward to getting on with your particular tasks. Several times over the next few weeks Al comes to you, and tells you that the program is "headed for disaster," and that there will probably be a layoff as a result. He also mentions that two of the other team members feel the project is a big waste of time. You ask Al for some specifics, but he says that he has been told these things "in confidence, and doesn't want to get anybody in trouble." What, if anything, are you going to do?

Chapter 7—Our Core Competencies & Strategic Intent

The Skill's Side of Job-effectiveness.

Early on it was suggested that an individual's job-effectiveness is built upon three fundamental components. Thus:

Job-effectiveness = Personal Work Ethics + Work Process + Acquired Vocational Skills.

So far, we have emphasized the first two components—the attitude and approach of a change agent. Now we must take a look at the third vital component of job-effectiveness —the unique skills that we are able to bring to bear in accomplishing a work task. After all, to recall our bad haircut analogy, it would be disastrous to be systematically coifed by a beautician, who exhibited high initiative and energy, if she did not have the requisite styling skills. So, we also need to take into careful account the level of excellence associated with our acquired vocational skills.

These are the skill sets in our personal toolboxes that differentiate a physician from a dentist, a journalist from a poet, and a fireman from a police officer. In a certain sense, these are the skills that tend to define ourselves as much as they define our job function. Generally, these professional skills depend on assimilating an organized body of knowledge that is learned through formalized courses at the university, technical school, or, perhaps through a defined apprentice program. Often, they are acquired through a combination of classroom learning and supervised training. We invest our time, hard work, and money to get these skills. And upon completion we receive a diploma, or some other form of pedigree certifying us as being a licensed psychologist, a certified public accountant, or a sworn police officer.

In order to be able to take stock of our individual vocational skills, we will employ two very insightful tools that were originally developed to help corporations improve their global competitiveness and establish market leadership. These are known respectively as Core Competencies and Strategic Intent[15], These tools were popularized in the early 1990's by two professors, C. K. Prahalad of the University of Michigan and Gary Hamel of the London School of Economics.

Interestingly, they work just as well at the "micro" level of the individual as they do at the "macro" level of the large organization. To understand why this is so, we will examine how they are used in the business environment, and then see how they can be applied to our own job situations.

Let us begin our study of core competencies with the following amusing little story of a fellow who wanted to do his job exceedingly well.

A DOG OF A STORY.

It seems that once there was a young man, just out of college, who aspired to quickly become a rich and famous writer. Through some influential friends of his father, he was able to meet jointly with three renowned publishers. For each he had but one question, "What kind of books sold best?" "Well," said the first publisher in his long experience, "stories about Abe Lincoln always seemed to do well." "Not quite right," insisted the second publisher, "doctor stories usually did much better." The third publisher had an entirely different opinion: "Everybody loves a dog story," she advised. After hurriedly thanking each of them for their advice, the young man rushed home to start his book about a dog that was owned by Abraham Lincoln's doctor!

The Evolution Of The Core Competency Concept.

There is a little bit of the thinking of that young man in all of us. In the job setting, we are often tempted to try and stake out the scope of our job activities, so that we can handle any situation. And until recently, many large corporations held to that same operating philosophy. In business, this approach is known as vertical integration, and it is driven by the seemingly sensible lure of having every base tagged. In other words, every enterprise would like to achieve a kind of invulnerable self-sufficiency.

Perhaps, Henry Ford I was the best known apostle of this approach as he built his automotive empire. Since engines were made of iron, and bodies of steel, Mr. Ford decided to invest in Minnesota iron ore mines. But, of course, he had to get the ore down to Detroit, which landed him in the Great Lakes shipping business. However, in order to convert the ore, Ford had to create a huge steel mill right beside his assembly lines at River Rouge, Michigan. Cars also needed window glass. So, old Henry set up a glass making plant in the same Rouge complex. But a car is useless without tires. This fact of life led him to invest in Indonesian rubber plantations in order to have a guaranteed source of tire material. Alas! What about a sure supply of leather for seats? Perhaps, he reasoned, he should go into the cattle raising business. But then there would be a new problem: What to do with all that meat?

It is not difficult to see where this "we-don't-want-to-depend-on-anybody-else" philosophy leads. It was hard for Ford to be giving his customers the kind of car styling, quality, and engineering improvements they wanted, when so much of his organization's energies were tied up in peripheral concerns, like the pros and cons of running a cattle ranch.

As global competition heated up in the early nineteen eighties many American companies had to come to grips with the mission–distracting and profit-eroding burdens of unbounded vertical integration. Each department, and each activity of a company, had to be re-examined to determine if in terms of quality and cost it met world-class standards.

For example, if a corporation manufactured home appliances, it had to ask itself whether or not it was cost efficient to maintain its own internal print shop for the instruction manuals shipped with each appliance. Or could the decorative trim on the appliances be produced on the outside at a lower cost or a higher quality? Further, should the appliance manufacturer continue to maintain its own individual retail outlet stores, or rely more on mass merchandisers such as Sears. Sears, on the other hand, had to take a hard look at its nearly century old catalogue business, and was forced to come to the conclusion that it could no longer compete effectively using this particular marketing strategy.

Thus, companies had to look themselves in the competitive mirror, and undertake a massive skills inventory. They needed to ask themselves two key questions:

1. What activities are vital to our mission?
2. In what activities are we really "world-class"?

The initially painful outcomes of this exercise, of course, were the many corporate "downsizings," or more euphemistically, "rightsizings," and the headline-grabbing job losses. But the intended benefit was the opportunity for companies to reposition themselves for sustained growth by focusing on what became known as their *core competencies*.

In their academic studies of core competency, Prahalad and Hamel presented evidence, which suggested that companies could significantly outgrow their competitors by continually exploiting those skill sets that met three fairly strict guidelines. These criteria were:

1. The skill sets were practiced to a level of excellence such that there were at most only a few competitive peers in a particular industry.
2. The company had found ways to exploit these sets of skills in multiple products and markets.
3. The company's customers recognized these skill sets as a source of real competitive advantage.

In a nutshell, the best way for a company to succeed was to "do more of what you already do best" [16] In the economic theory of international trade there is the Law of Comparative Advantage, which is based on similar criteria.

Perhaps, the best-known US corporation that has long followed a core competency philosophy is 3M. This company, which is widely admired for its constant flow of innovative new products, has a highly developed skill set of applying specialized coatings to papers and other substrates. Using this same basic competency, 3M produces such seemingly diverse products as Scotch Tape®, sandpaper, "Post-its"®, and magnetic recording tape. Actually, their list of products built on this competency numbers in the hundreds, and into markets we might not at first expect. For example, 3M uses this technology to make the skin–sticking electrodes used to hook-up patients to hospital EKG monitoring equipment.

Many companies have used the core competency approach to rethink the scope of their business activities. They have re-anchored their business along those activities at which they excel, can widely exploit in the marketplace, and have strong customer recognition.

Meeting this three-fold criteria is tough! Experience shows that core competencies develop only through the harmonious and long practiced learning of the organization. Because of this, experts are of the opinion that even large corporations rarely have more than a half dozen core competencies. Rightly then, core competencies have been called the "crown jewels" of an enterprise, and considerable organizational efforts go into protecting and enhancing them. When correctly and widely understood by management as true assets in the same sense as plant and equipment, the core competency philosophy has had the additional benefit of an upward valuing of the employees in whom these skill sets reside.

Discovering Our Individual Core Competencies.

Like companies, we might find, as we take a look at our individual skill sets, that some skills are practiced to such a level of excellence that they also deserve the recognition as being a core competence. And being able to widely exercise and further develop our unique core competencies is the key to continued, customer-valued job-effectiveness. In other words our customers feel they are getting the most bang for the buck. So, given the choice, we, as agents of change, would prefer to spend all of our work time exercising our core skills.

To determine if this is really the case, we can apply three tests that are quite similar to the ones companies use to identify their core competencies. Namely:

1. A skill set for which our level of excellence has few peers in our organization.
2. A professional competence that has broad applicability within our job scope or function.
3. A skill set for which our customers recognize a unique value.

As in the case of the large organization, the three core competency criteria are not easy to satisfy on a personal level. And we should not be surprised or disappointed, if we can only think of one or two as we take our skills inventory. Those just starting their careers may come up completely empty-handed; they are not likely to have either the practiced excellence or customer recognition that is required for a core. But as we will see in the following pages, even if we cannot identify a single core the first time around, taking a complete skills inventory is the key step in the evolution of our core competency seeds.

In taking this skills inventory we will find that in addition to whatever personal core competencies we may have, our job activities involve three other kinds of activities in varying degrees. These are:

1. Routine assignments which we will refer to as "do-lots-of's."
2. Applying certain specialized niche skills.
3. Developing skills to keep up with emerging needs.

Our Do-Lot's-of's Tasks: Necessary Or Force of Habit?

In the process of assessing their core competencies, companies have had to recognize that there are many functions in which they are heavily engaged, and which are necessary for the success of the organization, but at the same time they do not excel in terms of cost, quality, or technical leadership. These functions tend to fall into two classes: first there are the *sustaining* skills that directly support the making of the end products or services of the company. Secondly there are those activities that fall into the *organizational support* category. Some examples of sustaining skills might be routine metal stamping in a manufacturing company, or customer billing in a retail operation. The administration of health insurance and other employee benefits are examples of support functions that are needed in virtually any organization. We will refer to these non-core, sustaining and support activities as *do-lots-of's* .

In today's hyper-competitive, cost-sensitive world the corporate decision for both sustaining skills and support functions is essentially the same: either make the financial and time investments to bring them up to world class competitive standards, or outsource them wherever feasible to someone else who has reached this lofty plateau. The necessary decisions often do not come easy.

Similarly, on the personal level, whenever we take a look at how we end up spending our working days, we will invariably find that our jobs have many "do-lots-of's" associated with them. Doctors have lots of insurance forms to fill out; office assistants have lots of often-unread reports to distribute; and tradesmen spend lots of time running back and forth from one job site to another. These usually routine and often force-of-habit activities keep all of us from doing the really value creating work, that is rewarding both to our customers and ourselves. In other words, practicing our individual professional competencies.

However, by becoming consciously aware of our do-lots-of's, and the time required to perform them, we may be able to re-engineer our working routines to minimize this kind of activity. In this way we will then have more time to concentrate on and expand our truly professional cores.

Although it is obviously not possible to eliminate all of our do-lots-of's, they still need to be recognized as a frequent self-seductive lure that leads us to think that we are spending our work time profitably. We continue to do these assignments simply because we have always done them, and in a way even enjoy them. Instantaneously, reading and responding to e-mails in an almost Pavlovian fashion is a prime example. It is far more efficient to handle a collection of e-mails twice a day, than to allow ourselves to be constantly interrupted by a computer beep that conveys a kind of fire-alarm urgency.

Over-writing a simple inter office memo is another example of a seductive time-waster that falls into the do-lots-of category. It may be tempting to turn a simple complaint memo to the office supply department on the need to keep on hand a more generous supply of ballpoint pens into a Pulitzer prize-winning expose. But everyone understands the problems this causes without being lectured in hot and windy paragraphs about the inconvenience, aggravation, and loss of staff efficiency that a pen shortage causes. However, therapeutic this type of long memo may seem to us, it is in the end robbing ourselves of precious core time.

Niche Skills.

There is a particular category of skill sets that we might also find in taking our personal inventory. These are our *niche* skills. Niche skills are something that an organization or an individual does extremely well, but have at present only limited applicability. So, they fail one of the fundamental core competency tests—wide applicability. On the other hand, niche skills are often the seedlings of a personal core competency, and provide us with a visionary hint of what we as individuals might become.

By way of an actual example, early in his career as a purchasing agent, John volunteered to be on a team to re-layout a small engineering development facility. He enjoyed this assignment and demonstrated that he was especially effective in optimizing space utilization. As a result he was chosen to lead the team that planned a very major addition to the same facility a year later. Following the successful completion of this particular assignment, he was offered a corporate position to do this kind of job on a full time basis, at a time when his employer was expanding rapidly. Over a period of about ten years John had the opportunity to develop an ever-widening expertise in plant site selection, real estate valuations, and architectural negotiations on a national basis. Finally, he was made head of a large department with worldwide responsibilities for the overall planning, maintenance, and disposal of all building assets of that company. Thus, from an initial assignment a niche skill developed, which over time blossomed into a core competency. It, in turn, became the basis of a very rewarding career.

Every job-effective agent of change will encounter opportunities where his or her niche skills can be used to launch the development of a much more valuable core competency. So niche skills are not to be overlooked each time we update our personal inventory evaluation.

Emerging Needs.

If do-lots-of's represent a dangerous trap of eating up our most productive and rewarding work time, there is another non-core area where we are liable to have the opposite problem. It is a natural tendency to spend too little time in keeping ourselves current with the state-of-the-art in our chosen profession. Emerging needs sneak up on us slowly! For along time, we can find ways of getting our job done without them. So it is easy to put off developing the needed proficiency, and getting them into our toolbox. One day we wake up, however, only to find that these once emerging needs have moved up to the category of a required skill. They have become for us personally an obvious shortcoming. Certainly, the emergence of the computer as the basic working tool and communication means for virtually all workers is a dramatic example. Just think of the skill set differences between the "sixty words per minute, accurate typist" who was sought after twenty years ago, and the word processing expert of today. Who is going to get the job now?

Likewise picture the difference between the draftsman of your Dad's era with his "T Square," triangles, and ink pens with today's software-sophisticated computer-aided design operator.

These two examples point-out another important, but less happy, aspect of our hard-won core competencies: Their fortunes are inextricably bound up with the dynamic of enterprise itself. Changes in technology, market needs, or competitive forces continually erode their value. In some fast-moving technology fields such as solid state electronics, engineers speak of having a half-life of from four to seven years. By this it is meant that fifty percent of what they learned in school becomes obsolete over that time frame. It is as if they were carrying around their technical skills in a very leaky bucket.

Similarly, medical schools recognize this same dynamic. They typically include in their mission statement words to the effect: "Our purpose is to provide our students with the academic foundation for a *lifelong study* of the medical sciences." Agents of change are by definition life-long learners!

So, in order to maintain our competence–based job-effectiveness, each of us must be prepared to look carefully into our toolboxes. We must be prepared to throw out those old outdated tools, and spend some quality time replenishing them with new ones. We do this by periodically identifying and nurturing our *emerging needs.*

Putting Together The Overall Picture.

Now that we have distinguished four different kinds of job activities that make up the inventory of our individual job profiles, we need to have a convenient way of seeing the total picture and the inter-relationships of these job activities. A four-quadrant chart, such as illustrated in Figure 7.1, can serve very well as a kind of job assessment mirror. Here, we have created a set of linked boxes that split our job efforts into the four categories we have just defined. Notice the boxes are arranged vertically to reflect the relative value to our customers, and horizontally to reflect the relative amounts of time we might typically spend working in each category. That is, ordinarily most of our work efforts go into pursuing our core competencies and fulfilling our do-lots-of's obligations, while relatively little time is devoted to emerging needs and niche skills. Our job-effectiveness aim, of course, is to spend as much of our working time in those high customer value quadrants of core competency and niche skills as we possibly can. At the same time we want to minimize the "do-lots-of's," and show due consideration for our emerging needs, which will provide customer value in the future. In Figure 7.1, there are suggested ranges of job time we might try to devote to each box. These ranges point out the dilemma all of us face: it is simply not possible to spend 70% of our time working on our core competencies, 10% doing some niche activities, and 15% learning something new, if our do-lots-of's are consuming half of our work time. Clearly some tradeoffs are continually being called for. Here is one sure tip-off of a job-effective change agent: they have developed a facility, which borders on an instinct, to keep their time-wasting do-lots-of's to an absolute minimum!

Taking Stock Of Our Own Job Activities. To analyze our individual job-effort profiles, we need to draw-up a four-quadrant chart identical to Figure 7.1. Then, we have to spend some time thinking about the various tasks we typically perform in a working month, and list them under the appropriate headings. We will also want to estimate how much of our time is spent in each of the four categories Finally, we want to come up with a plan that more favorably alters the balance.

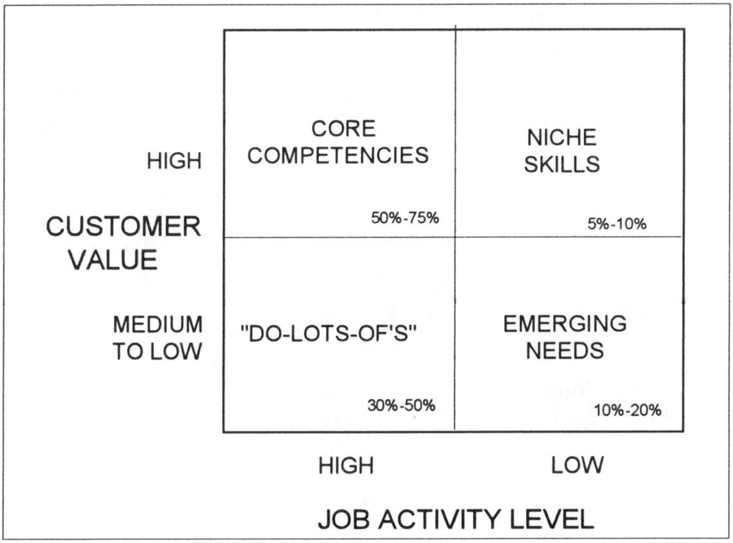

Figure 7.1. Use Of A Quadrant Chart To Illustrate Relative Value To Customers of Job Activities.

Let us deal with the do-lots-of's first. Here is where some re-engineering can have some big payoffs! For example, in the case of an office assistant, she may still have some secretarial "baggage" hanging around from the old days. So, she might still spend a lot of time cleaning up memos and reports prior to distribution, answering the phone, or making travel arrangements. Routinely performing these tasks for a large office staff can easily add up to a full time job. But with some skillful negotiations, she may be able to change the culture so that everybody routinely runs their memos through a computer spell-check, answers their own phone, or calls the travel agency directly.

Next, as we take stock of our job situation, the thought may occur to us that we have one or two niche type skills. Instead of a specific niche skill, perhaps, there are a few special assignments that we are periodically asked to take on.

For example, maybe for the last four years the management has asked us to organize and run the annual United Fund Drive. Or it may be that we have been selected to represent our department whenever next-generation information processing equipment and software are being selected.

As a third step of the job inventory process, we will want to list our emerging needs in the appropriate box. If we have trouble identifying some emerging needs, it is a safe bet to put down "update computer/ software skills." No matter what our profession, it is not likely that we will be wrong!

Once we have charted our do-lots-of's, niche skills and emerging needs, we can put down our core competencies. Core competencies should not take long to figure out. All we need to do is to apply the three tests of performance excellence, broad applicability, and customer recognition. If we identify more than a few cores, we are probably being to easy on ourselves.

What might be a little difficult is the next step: putting down on the chart the relative amounts of working time we spend in each quadrant. Difficult because if we are going to derive any value from this exercise we need to list the actual amount of time spent as opposed to what we wished would be the case. Unfortunately, many people painfully find themselves prime downsizing candidates, or on the way to "burn-out," as they confront too late the fact that nearly one hundred percent of their very hard work efforts are in the relatively low-valued do-lot's-of category.

The four-quadrant chart paints for us an up-to-date picture of our job activities, which we can use to realistically gauge our current job-effectiveness. But as we will see in the example charts below, it often suggests a plan on how we might eliminate many do-lots-of's, and use our emerging needs and niche skills to further our core competency development.

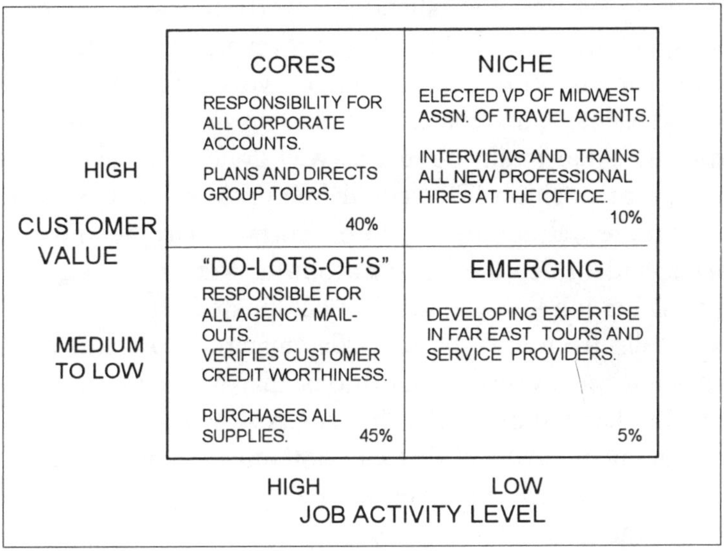

Figure 7.2. Job Quadrant Chart For Travel Agent.

A Look At Two Job Quadrant Charts

Mary is a forty-some college grad, married, and living in a major Midwestern city. She has been employed as a senior travel agent for a medium-sized firm during the last five years. The job skill quadrant chart she has put together is shown in Figure 7.2.

After studying Mary's chart for a little bit, we might first notice that Mary seems to have some definite managerial talent based on her two listed niche skills as an elected officer in her industry association, and in her interviewing and training inter-actions with the agency's new hires. Next, we notice that Mary's core skills are ones that are likely to have high impact on the agency's sales growth and profits—the arrangement of group tours and the responsibility for the lucrative corporate travel accounts. These are some sure signs of a highly experienced travel agent.

Judging by Mary's estimate of forty-five percent of her time spent on her do-lots-of's, however, she seems to be bogged down with routine office work. There are some activities—mail-outs and the purchasing of office supplies, in particular—that might be just as well done by somebody in a more junior position. This could free up Mary to concentrate on her more value-creating core efforts. Lastly, we note that Mary has identified the Far East tour market as an area, which she feels her job knowledge must be updated.

Overall, from this basic skills inventory breakdown we have some pretty good indications that Mary is a seasoned "pro. She has the drive and the talents to work at the level of a change agent. A level that can potentially benefit Mary, her customers, and her employer, assuming she can work her way out of some of the do-lots-of's.

****

Frank is a thirty-year old history instructor at a small college. He has just completed the first of a three-year teaching contract. His current job inventory chart is illustrated by Figure 7.3. Frank, as a result of his Ph.D. studies and publication activities, has developed a core competency in European Renaissance history, an obviously specialized area of expertise. And one that is most likely to have any real customer-recognized value only in the environs of a large university.

Unfortunately, his current teaching responsibilities, which absorb 65% of his work time, seem to be taking him in the wrong direction. Frank finds himself with a fairly heavy teaching load—three classes of mandatory American History, and an Introductory Sociology course to boot—at an institution where his core skills are playing no major role. These teaching assignments might even have low to medium value to his student-customers, simply because this is not Frank's area of expertise, or perhaps even interest.

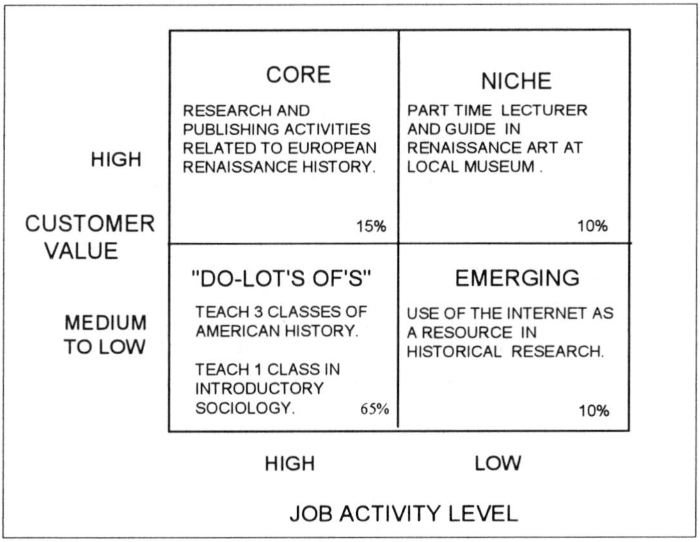

Figure 7.3. Job Quadrant For Frank, A Renaissance History Expert.

From his core competency and niche skill listings, it appears that Frank is trying to at least keep his core skills alive by writing and serving as a Renaissance Art lecturer at a downtown museum. But together they only absorb 25% of his work time. In fact, his core competency area does not currently even come close to meeting the requirement of broad applicability. Lastly, in preparing his skills inventory, Frank has recognized that computer methodologies and the Internet have become increasingly useful tools in carrying out historical research. So, he has determined to master these technologies as a way of enhancing his core competency bucket.

Let's put ourselves in Frank's shoes for a moment, and decide what he should do as far as his career based on his professional skills inventory. The obvious scenario we might portray based on his chart seems like a rather bleak one—Frank is simply stuck in the wrong job for the next couple of years! But on further thought there might be another way to look at Frank's situation that will lead to a much happier outcome. Suppose he saw a way to turn his current predicament to advantage with the following thoughts:

"My real career goal is to teach Renaissance History at the university level, but there are only a few jobs available in this rather specialized field. To get this kind of position, I must demonstrate that I have experience in teaching, which is backed up with some solid recommendations. So, my plan is to secure a university appointment after these two years. In the meantime, I will continue with my present teaching assignments. By really putting my heart into it, I can accumulate some good faculty and student performance ratings. Besides, lecturing at the Art Museum keeps me up to date in my specialty. I will also use this time to write a few papers on the use of the Internet in historical research that I can get published in the Journal of History. This will help me to broaden my reputation in the field."

"I can also use this time to re-layout a new course syllabus on Renaissance history, which I intend to send along with my resume when I apply at various universities. After all, not many students elect a course in Renaissance History because they think it is boring and irrelevant. I think a totally new approach to presenting this kind of material is needed, and I think I know how to do that..."

Now Frank is beginning to talk like a change agent! As we can see from the above example, whether or not Frank sees himself dead in the water for the near term, or at the gateway to a highly satisfying career, all depends on his long range plan or strategy. The business term for this long range goal planning is called Strategic Intent, an empowering concept, which we will now explore.

Mapping Out Our Strategic Intent.

In the corporate realm Strategic Intent has a fairly precise and technical meaning. But for our personal purposes we can define it as a *driving obsession to achieve a lofty and distant goal along our career paths.* So, the first thing we have to do is to develop, and over time whole-heartedly embrace, the visionary goal that we equate with our career destiny.

For some of us, discovering this goal is as simple as asking ourselves "What is it we would like to be when we grow-up?" So, we tell ourselves that we want to become a surgeon, a writer, or a news anchorman. For many others, it is expressed in terms of being the best performer in an already chosen field. Thus our vision might be to become the best violinist in the Chicago Symphony Orchestra, or the most knowledgeable research librarian in the State of Missouri. It is a situation where "different strokes for different folks" applies, and your career Strategic Intent is that particular *worthy* goal that happens to turn you on.

Running The Marathon.

The real value of formulating a personal strategic intent is its long-term motivational effect as we progress through a sequence of often difficult steps in trying to achieve a worthy end goal. Some people like to think of this overarching plan as a kind of personalized marathon race that has been broken down into four hundred-meter segments.

Suppose, a young woman has always dreamed of becoming a surgeon. If she is not obsessed with the idea, it is the next closest thing! She reads everything she can get her hands on about medicine, and watches every "doctor" program there is on television. She is sure that she wants to take "pre-med" when she enters college next fall.

It's a long haul from being a freshman in college to a practicing surgeon; four years of college, four years of medical school, and then a grueling residency of five years. It is certainly a worthy and reaching objective, so it meets our definition of a Strategic Intent. But lots of times, just thinking of the whole jaunt is enough to scare this young lady away. So, from now on she decides she just won't. Instead, she senses that she is in a kind of marathon, and the first lap is to get an "A" in freshman chemistry. Then there will be a lap or two to get top grades in physics and biochemistry. Next, she will find herself running a couple more really uphill laps getting ready for the exams to be accepted into a medical school.

She won't believe she could learn so much material in the first-year lap through medical school. Then one day in her third year, when she will really feel tired by the whole experience, she will receive an unexpected burst of energy: a patient seeing her in a long white lab coat will mistakenly, but rewardingly, call her "doctor." Now, this woman will finally know that the Strategic Intent she committed to long ago is going to be a reality, even though there are still some long laps to go.

Writing Our Strategic Intent Chapter By Chapter.

Perhaps another way of formulating our individual Strategic Intent is to think of it in much the same way as if we were starting to write a three hundred-page book. If we just sat down and started to write, it is likely that by the time we had finished page twenty-six, all we would be thinking about was that there were still two hundred and seventy four pages to go! Even worse, we would suddenly remember that there are about two hundred and fifty words to a page. We would be wondering, "How much is two hundred fifty times two hundred seventy four?" No matter how enthused or knowledgeable we were on our subject matter, there is a good possibility we would decide right then and there to give the whole project up!

On the other hand, if we first prepared a rough outline of all the various topics we wanted to cover, and then grouped the topics around a dozen chapters, we would find that we had a much more doable situation on our hands. We could then timeline our efforts by committing to write one chapter per month. And with reasonable dedication have a good assurance that our book would be done in, say, a year. Strategic Intent is best achieved by outlining our career plans, one chapter at a time.

Think Strategic Intent First; Rewards Second.

We deserve to be rewarded for our hard work efforts. But it is important not to put the cart before the horse, when it comes to substituting the personal rewards that are expected to flow from a well chosen Strategic Intent with the Strategic Intent itself. Strategic Intent motivates us to take the difficult but sure path to accomplishment, while an undue, upfront focus on the rewards tempts us to take some "iffy" shortcuts.

Corporations, for example, sometimes try to define "what-they-want-to-be-when-they-grow-up" in lucrative dollar terms. So, they will cast their driving vision in words such as, "We will increase our return on shareholder equity from the current twelve percent to eighteen percent over the next three years." The achievement of rewarding financial goals is, indeed, a prime responsibility of the management of the enterprise. But this is the kind of "Strategic Intent," whose meaning most of their employees will not even comprehend, much less become obsessed with achieving. Far better, and paradoxically, much more likely of achieving big financial rewards, would be a stated vision expressed along the lines, "Within three years, our Strategic Intent is to have every major customer in the aerospace industry rank us number one in terms of product quality, delivery and service." In this case, every engineering, sales, manufacturing floor, and shipping department employee has a guiding sense of the management's values, and what they should strive for each day as they perform their particular job.

In the same way, if we plan to be an anchorman, our focus has to be on the creation of riveting newscast stories as we wind our way through a Journalism curriculum; not the red Ferrari convertible we will someday drive home from the TV station. We need a Strategic Intent to keep us pushing for an "A" in our Communication classes, not another daydream!

Changing Our Lap Strategies.

Strategic Intent is by its very nature a form of long-range planning. But it is not a one-time event, rather, it is a living plan! Whenever, we change employers, take on significantly different job responsibilities, or get bored with what we are doing, it is certainly time to rethink the "marathon" and how we intend to run the next couple laps.

Occasionally, we might even find that we have been running in the wrong race all along. We come to recognize that we are not fulfilling that quintessential dream of what we want to be when we grow up. So, we may even need to layout a new Strategic Intent, lap by lap. Far better to do that than stay in a race we have no real desire to win.

Strategic Intent is one of those occasionally used, but very useful tools in our job-effective toolbox. It provides us with a motivating theme in the form of a worthy career goal. At the same time, it helps us to organize our careers in the form of flexible and manageable chapters, each of which sequentially brings the achievement of that desired goal one step closer.

An Integrated View of Core Competencies And Strategic Intent.

An analysis of our core competencies, using the job quadrant chart, helps us to identify our current *performance gap.* It tells us what we need to do to become job-effective change agents in our present position. Strategic Intent, on the other hand, provides us with the complementary input of helping us to pinpoint our *opportunity gap*. In other words, it provides us with a forward vision of all that we might still become. It is the long-range plan of the agent of change to create beneficial change for himself or herself. So, with Strategic Intent there is the idea of stretching or leveraging our current capabilities. While core competency analysis causes us to focus on our *resources* to achieve a present result, Strategic Intent puts the emphasis on our *resourcefulness* to attain a future goal.

It has been said that the management of an enterprise has a three-fold responsibility:

1. Optimize the present.
2. Actively create the future.
3. Selectively forget the past.

This advice is an equally good checklist for change agents, as they continually rebalance their own work activities. It is the dynamic underlying job-effectiveness. We are optimizing the present when we concentrate our efforts on our core personal competencies. We are creating our futures when we expand our niche skills, and address our emerging needs in a way that is consistent with our Strategic Intent. And we selectively forget the past when we make every effort to minimize our do-lots-of's, especially those seductive ones that for whatever reason of comfort, security, or past success we are reluctant to give up. Lastly, it will be recognized that an analysis of our core competencies and strategic intent are good examples in themselves of the job-effective work process of gathering, evaluating and then implementing a beneficial change. It is a self-adaptive change in which we become our own customer.

Discussion Problems.

1. Prepare your own job quadrant chart using the four categories of core competencies, do-lots-of's, emerging needs, and niche skills. What percentage of time is spent in each? Is the picture that emerges consistent with your long-term goals? If not what has to change?

2. If your customers were asked, which core competencies would they associate with you?

3. Develop an action plan to cut your do-lots-of's by 50 percent over the next year. Take a very hard look at those activities that give you some sense of comfort or security.

4. Write down your personal strategic intent. How far are you along in running this marathon? What must you do to successfully complete the next lap?

5. How might the job quadrant chart be useful in counseling a hard working subordinate with a performance problem in getting customer-valued results?

Chapter 8— The Knowledge Worker As Change Agent

Computer Literacy: Admission Ticket To The 21st Century.

At the turn of the century, there is little of social and economic consequence that has not been profoundly impacted by computer technology and the Internet. Indeed, one has to reach back more than a hundred years to the explosive and pervasive application of electrical power to find anything comparable. Electrification provided wall-socket convenience to effortlessly power countless physical tasks, whether at home or at work. In the same way, the Internet provides wall-socket convenience to a far superior power—the power to be *informed.* And the PC itself has evolved to become the motor that transforms this power into a quantum jump in our overall job-effectiveness.

Doctors now search the Internet worldwide for diagnostic and treatment information on obscure illnesses. So do their patients. Lawyers comprehensively find their case precedents via the keyboard, instead of laborious manual searches of dusty law volumes. Key components for jumbo jets are computer designed simultaneously by engineers in half a dozen different countries, and their inter-actions are simulated over the Internet. Skilled machinists now software program their lathes and milling machines to efficiently produce dozens of parts, rather than manually guide their work pieces one at a time, as in the past. Students, as early as the first grade, explore enormously expanded worlds of arts and sciences by tapping into the Internet. Even churches now use this medium in their missionary search to save souls.

Internet commerce is a revolution in its own right. People buy, or more accurately make bids on, everything from stocks to vacations and cars via the Internet. AOL rivals ATT in name recognition in just five years rather than a hundred. Wall Street drives itself into a feeding frenzy to devour the stock of any company with ".com" in its name, sometimes making Internet entrepreneurs billionaires in a single trading day.

Dollar measures of the Internet's rocketing growth are all but incomprehensible. In 1994 the total Internet economy was estimated to be less than $5 billion dollars annually. A survey by the University of Texas put the 1998 figure at $301 billion. Pointedly the same survey indicated that Internet related jobs accounted for 1.2 million new jobs; roughly 40% of the US total new job creation for 1998! And what can we expect for the future? Well, according to the experts, they foresee anywhere between a 1.3 and a 5.0 trillion-dollar Internet economy by the year 2003.[17]

Why this phenomenal growth in computer technology and its ultimate expression, the Internet? The reason is that the computer-based Internet has become the global village's master communications link, as well as the world's main public library of data and information. The latter a truly global and dynamically living library that contains, with only slight exaggeration, virtually all the available data and information on practically any subject in the world. What is more, all this data and information can be accessed nearly instantaneously anywhere, and at anytime, for little or no cost, with just a few strokes of a keyboard or clicks of a mouse.

The Computer/Internet Redefines the Meaning of Job-Effectiveness.

In our discussion of the process of work, we identified three sequential steps—gathering, evaluating, and implementing—that form the foundation for any beneficial change. The computer/Internet revolution greatly expands our capabilities in the gathering and evaluating phases of this three-step work process. This expansion is two dimensional in nature. We gather the needed data and evaluate the resultant information much quicker, yet far more thoroughly. So much so, as to cause a major re-sizing in today's accepted standards for worker productivity. Most significantly, while the job-effectiveness of workers who possess computer and Internet skills has been greatly enhanced, in stark contrast, those who lack them are becoming increasingly disenfranchised. Truly, the digital divide grows ever wider!

The Computer/Internet in the Workplace.

Once we have come to understand the capabilities of this extraordinary technology, and have developed a user-friendliness with the computer itself, we can better appreciate the job-effective power it can provide us as agents of change. We do this by looking closely at the way people succeed in the world of providing goods and services ninety-five percent of the time. Nearly always, we take something that already exists in the market place in some form, and improve it in a way that makes it *quicker, better,* or *cheaper*. Indeed, some very famous companies have built much of their business strategy around developing a market reputation for excelling at being quicker, better or cheaper than their competitors. Federal Express, Mercedes, and Wal Mart are outstanding examples of each of these different strengths respectively.

Earlier, the "Q-B-C" spaghetti test was introduced as a useful way of making sure our work product is of benefit to a customer. Well, here it comes up again! And figuring out how to make something quicker, better or cheaper does depend a lot on having superior, up-to-the-minute *data* and *information.* In other words, once the need for the product or service has been established in the market place, what is necessary for the next generation success depends in large measure on having timely access to all the available facts and figures that pertain to that product or service.

Making Widgets Quicker, Better, And Cheaper.

Let's look at a typical work place example. Suppose your company is in the business of making "widgets" along with three other manufacturers. Let's assume the widgets from all four suppliers are pretty much the same, and sell for close to the same price. Maybe your boss decides that your company is no longer going to be satisfied with an equal twenty five percent share of the overall market. So you, as the assigned change agent, start pursuing the Q-B-C strategy over the Internet.

First, you might find out through some detailed searching over the world wide web that the key materials required for making widgets are available from twenty one different vendors. You also determine that material costs could be reduced twenty percent by buying some key components from an offshore supplier—Hong Kong Metals. You not so casually mention this in a conversation an hour later with your present supplier, Acme Steel. "What a coincidence," Al, the Acme salesman blurts-out, "We were planning to offer you the very same deal starting tomorrow!"

Next, by initiating a second search you might find data from the National Association of Retail Merchants that provides statistical data indicating that 80% of all widgets are bought by women. This starts you thinking that maybe it would make sense to make your widgets with a little more feminine appeal. Perhaps, you could supply them in a color other than the drab olive that your company has been using ever since it was awarded an Army contract twenty years ago. So you search the worldwide web again using the key words "FASHIONABLE COLORS." And lo and behold, you get a "hit" that tells you that the American Academy of Fashion Designers has just completed a survey indicating that fuchsia is going to be very big this fall. "But what in the world is fuchsia?" you ask yourself. After a quick check of your computer's Thesaurus software you learn that fuchsia is somewhere between purple and red. So, you decide to bet on fuchsia paint.

Now you have a product that you think can be made more appealing with fuchsia, and made cheaper by having scared Acme Steel with data on competitive sources. But what about being quicker? From your company's computer database you know that 60% of the sales of your widgets are sold in the Western United States; the trouble is that your manufacturing plant happens to be in Maine. Moreover, the Western Region sales manager insists he could increase sales of widgets another forty percent if it did not take an average of two weeks for customers to receive them by rail.

Given this information, you begin to mull over in your mind a series of alternatives. With the help of some readily available modeling software, called "E-Z Paybak" you explore alternatives such as:

(1) Investing the capital to build a second plant on the West Coast.
(2) Licensing somebody else to manufacture widgets in California.
(3) Paying the extra costs to ship the widgets from Maine by Air Express.

Quickly, the computer grinds through the three alternatives and the many cost variables that affect their relative outcomes. Let us assume that the "E-Z Paybak" analysis indicates that the capital costs are too high to build a second plant; there is not enough profit margin to split with a manufacturing licensee; and air freighting from Maine looks like the best alternative.

Notice how in the above example the Internet has been used to gather some of the facts needed to make our widgets cheaper and better. And the computer with the "E-Z Paybak" software has been employed to evaluate some of the alternative "what-ifs" of getting the product in the hands of the customers more rapidly. In a real life situation there might be dozens of variables involved. Interest rates, packaging expenses, insurance costs, warehousing charges, and legal fees to name just a disparate few. But so long as we can identify these variables and plug them into the program we can depend on the computer to tirelessly and accurately plow through the tediously complex calculations to give us the optimum answer.

This synergistic combination, which takes advantage of the computer's superb ability to manipulate data and the Internet's unmatched capabilities to access information, are the key reasons why a worker's output in terms of speed and thoroughness can be so much greater today.

What The Computer/ Internet Can't Do.

As important as quick access and comprehensiveness of information are in the workplace, we must not make the mistake of seeing it as the whole story. They are the building blocks but not the whole of job-effectiveness. To understand why this is so, it is helpful to look at the distinct roles that data, information, and knowledge play in the process of creating beneficial change.

In everyday speech we tend to use the words, *data, information,* and *knowledge* rather interchangeably. So whether somebody tells us that they have data, information or knowledge about next Tuesday's weather forecast, we are not generally troubled by seemingly subtle shades in their meaning. The message we are looking for is that rain is expected, or that it is not. However, when we talk about computers and how we humans interact with them, these three words are really worth fussing about. Although the Internet and computer are the hands down winner when it comes to gathering *data,* and presenting this data in the form of useful *information,* they can't hold a candle to us humans when it comes to operating on this information to create useful *knowledge*.

Data, Information and Knowledge: There Really Is a Difference!

For our present purposes, let us define data to be a *collection of facts that are presumed to be true*. As the example in Figure 8.1 indicates, if we surveyed the heights of a handful of college students we would have some data. By measuring the heights of many students and organizing this data in some meaningful way we would start to develop information. *Information is data that has been codified or structured in some way* so that we can get our arms around it. Rather than trying to comprehend a ten-page list of the names of all the students and their heights on it, we find it far easier to make sense of a statement such as, "One hundred percent of all persons measured have heights between five foot two inches and six foot six inches."

But now lets pin down our definition of knowledge. Knowledge is *developed information that we couple with theories, past experience, and judgments to obtain useful results.* Suppose our job is to design the height of the doors for a new college dormitory. The information we obtained from our survey tells us that all the people measured are less than six foot six. But our past experience with survey data tells us that we ought to be a bit cautious. Does a survey of three hundred students really portray a university population of twenty-five thousand? Statistical theory tells us that there is very likely to be some plus or minus error. Besides, we *know* people often wear hats in the winter, and girls sometimes wear high heels on special dates. So, maybe we ought to add an extra six inches to be sure nobody loses their hat or bangs their head.

Upon further reflection we decide we better scan the names on the data list, and just as we suspected, we find that none of the varsity basketball team participated in the survey. So in the process of specifying a final door height we *decide* to add an extra twelve inches rather than six.

	**"Data"** is a collection of facts presumed to be true.	John is 5' 8" tall. Mary is 5'11" tall. Ted is 6' 2" tall.
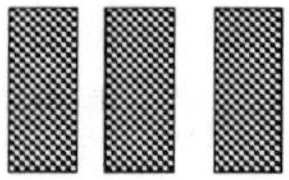	**"Information"** is data that has been organized in some understandable way.	All students surveyed are between 5'2" and 6' 6" in height.
	**"Knowledge"** is information coupled with theories, past experience and judgments to obtain a useful result.	"If we make the doorways 7' 6" in height we can take care of everybody even if they wear a hat."

Figure 8.1, The Relationship Between Data, Information, And Knowledge.

Knowledge: Where We Win Out!

Notice our final answer on the proper door height came about by *recalling a* well-established theoretical concept that there will always be some error in statistical data. Also, we *know from experience*, that hats and high heels need to be taken into account. And finally, after some *reflection,* we *suspected* that some very tall people were left out of the survey. The words italicized above give us hints of what we mean by the powerful and uniquely human process called knowledge generation.

Dr. Harold Barrows, a neurologist, educator, and writer on the knowledge process, refers collectively to these powerful and uniquely human pondering capabilities as "metacognition, ... the executive function in thinking."[18] Still, another authority in the field, R. Schön captures the essence of this knowledge generating capability with the thought that it is the "skillful holding of a conversation with a problem."

Can we ever imagine a computer conversing with itself, thinking about hats and heels, or being a little bit suspicious about the data it just generated? Certainly not with today's technology, however reaching. It is between *information* and *knowledge* that we encounter the wide, and perhaps forever, unbridgeable chasm between machine and man. A gulf as wide as a software program is from the human soul. Computers and the Internet excel at informing us of *what-is-now.* But it is the mind of man starting with what-is-now that makes that enormous leap to *what-can-be*. What-can-be is the essence of that beneficial change process we call progress. It is also the limitless workspace of the agent of change.

As illustrated by the example survey of student heights, we must always guard against mistaking limited data for complete information. So too, at the other end of the spectrum, there is a like danger in equating very complete information for true knowledge. It is true that computers have already been "taught" enough programming to be able to beat the world's best players in the game of chess. These super-computers excel at exhausting all the possible moves and counter-moves by blindly following, albeit with nanosecond speed, their man-determined instructions. But there is not a computer in the world that is capable of thinking-up the game of chess, or even suggesting that it might be fun to play a game this evening. Thus, the real power of the computer and Internet lies not with the lightning fast microprocessor, or the vast storehouses of newly accessible information. Rather, it is those slow moving fingers operating the keyboard!

The Growing Need For Knowledge Workers.

As the impact of the information age has become more and more pervasive, we have begun to hear correspondingly more about the need for "knowledge workers" A knowledge worker is defined as a person, who:

1. Gathers data or information from any source.
2. Adds value to the information.
3. Distributes these value-added information products to others.[19]

Note that this definition of the task approach to knowledge work is one that closely parallels our three-step work process of creating beneficial change.

The Characteristics of Knowledge Work.

Knowledge work tends to have a distinct set of characteristics that are quite different than say the repetitive factory assembly line jobs and their front office equivalents of just twenty-five years ago. To the greatest extent possible, everything was done in those times to take any sort of independent thinking out of the job. Factory people had their simplified line instructions from which they dare not deviate, and the office staff had their standard procedures, from which their decisions would also not dare deviate. Knowledge work changes that paradigm completely!

The essence of knowledge work is *independent decision making* that is characterized by:

1. Complexity.
2. A cyclical working process.
3. Inherent variability.
4. The need for collaboration.
5. The risk of failure.
6. The need for remote trust.

Let us look at these characteristics in a little more detail.

Complexity.

Products today are complex, often involving mechanisms, electronics, and software within a single package. Services are equally intricate involving multi-mode distribution channels, myriad governmental regulations, and cost structures. And indeed, so too are the complexities of the jobs of the people who make these products and services happen. Many, frequently conflicting issues have to be addressed and resolved if an optimum decision is to be reached. Usually there are many potential ways to solve the same problem, each of which must be explored in greater or lesser degree.

We have no difficulty understanding this characteristic for neurosurgeons and tax lawyers. But consider, for example, the knowledge complexity inherent in the following four jobs that we might be initially inclined to think of as being "hands-on":

1. Farmer: Needs broad knowledge of soils and soil mechanics; fertilizers and pesticides; crop characteristics and rotations; machinery operation and repair; financing and futures markets.

2. Police Officer: Demands extensive knowledge of criminal, civil, and traffic enforcement laws; arrest procedures and citizen rights; criminology and evidence collection, weaponry and martial arts.

3. Factory Technician: Requires understanding of the operation, adjustment, and repair of automation assembly equipment involving complex mechanisms and electronics; interpretation of statistical process control charts; and the use of sophisticated instruments and gauges.

4. Licensed Chef: Involves broad understanding of nutritional and flavor characteristics of meats and fish, fruits and vegetables, breads and desserts. Must understand sourcing, selection and efficient preparation of various food types, along with cultural history and table presentation.

Cyclical Work Process.

Paradoxically, as our knowledge develops of a situation so does our comprehension of the depths of our ignorance. This causes a constant need to cycle back by uncovering more data, and developing more information. In this way we create a comfort level that an optimum decision can be achieved. In the work setting the task of achieving a beneficial change is most often presented to us in the form of a vaguely defined problem to be solved. For example, "Relative to our competitors, our overhead expenses here at Baker Machine Bolt Company are too high. We must reduce these costs significantly!" Now if you were assigned this or any similar problem your state of knowledge would probably proceed through three distinct phases:

Stage 1. *What you don't know is what you don't know.* Unless you happened to be the company controller you would probably have a rather incomplete idea of which employees, departments, and outside services were lumped into the "overhead" account. But soon you would start to gather data from a variety of sources in and outside the company of what functions typically comprise overhead. After a good deal of effort you would come up with information in the form of a fairly comprehensive list of overhead accounts. Still, you might find that you are missing a lot of data regarding how much money each account cost the company per year. This would bring your knowledge state to the second stage.

Stage 2. *You know what information you do not possess, but still need to solve the problem.* By the time you arrive at stage 2, you start to feel that you are gaining control of the situation. You understand what it will take to solve the problem, and now its more a matter of putting forward the required effort to assemble the needed data. Let us say in this case, that it is office supplies, charitable donations, and expenses for travel and entertainment.

Stage 3. *You know that you know.* You are confident that you have all the information needed to exercise your judgment and come to a sound decision. Your organized information tells you that expenses for office supplies and charitable donations are well within budget. But on the average each salesman is spending in excess of ten percent of the sales dollars on travel and entertainment. For a company making and selling machine bolts that seems way too high! Your own judgment and the experience of others tell you that two or three percent would be a lot more reasonable.

Now you are in a position to take appropriate action by implementing a beneficial change. Let's say you decide to implement a policy that:

1. States that travel and entertainment expenses will not on the average exceed 3% of sales.
2. Requires each salesman to report his "T&E" expenses weekly until the situation is fully under control.

Inherent Variability.

Today's problem, even if it is of the same genre, is always some how different than yesterday's. There will be a new environmental regulation, a better antibiotic, a new shipping rate structure, or a new competitor on the scene. Each of these will challenge the agent of change to come up with a totally different approach. Likewise, in the realm of providing goods and services, the one-shoe-fits-all approach to doing business has simply gone out the window with the demands of "mass-customization." We need to be able to supply each customer with a tailored product or service to meet his or her precise desires, while at the same time, doing so in a cost efficient and rapid manner.

Need for Collaboration, Risk of Failure, And Remote Trust

The need for collaboration, the risk of failure, and an organizational culture of remote trust come part and parcel with knowledge work. Complexity of products and services demands the collaborative efforts of many for success. No one individual has all the answers in today's work world. As we have previously seen in our discussion of Problem Based Learning, the cycling back and forth process, which is typical of knowledge generation, is much more productive when attacked on a team basis.

For parallel reasons, the possibility of failure with any product, service, or, for that matter, any customer-desired beneficial change increases exponentially with the associated complexity and variability of the required task. Thus, endeavors rooted in knowledge-based activities often involve some degree of risk. Moreover, the expansive and often uncharted nature of knowledge work demands a corresponding degree of what has been aptly termed "remote trust" on the part of a management. The roving eye of the traditional supervisor simply can no longer dependably cover the landscape. Management must be willing to risk failure. Indeed, even on occasion rewarding early failures in the spirit of "lessons-learned," and in encouraging a quick switch to a more promising approach.

Needless to say, a sense of remote trust and the concomitant tolerance of failure come hard for traditional hierarchical organizations, whose very structure is predicated on the prevention, and sometimes even the punishment of mistakes. Unfortunately, in today's fast-paced marketplace, where being there first is often the surest guarantee of long-term success, the line between managerial caution and paralyzing inaction has become ever more narrow.

Knowledge Workers As Change Agents.

It has been pointed out how the task approach of the knowledge worker matches closely the three-step work process of a change agent. When we further consider the nature of knowledge work, it is also easy to see how the "sixpack" work ethic of a change agent fulfills the needed attitudes of a job-effective knowledge worker. A high degree of initiative and credibility are the quid pro quo that brings about management's remote trust. Self-adaptability guards us against the overly long pursuit of a doomed approach. Lastly, the complexity, variability, and cyclicality inherent in knowledge work will provide daily tests of a worker's energy and senses of commitment and follow-up. The knowledge worker whose "value added" work output results in customer-desired beneficial change is indeed a true agent of change.

Most Jobs Of The Future Will Be Filled by Knowledge Workers.

We have seen previously that three-quarters of the labor force is devoted to service work. It is further estimated that 75% of all service workers, today, are knowledge workers; a percentage which is still gaining.[20] In fact, spurned on by the information revolution, some would prefer to refer to the New Economy as the *Knowledge Economy* where information increasingly displaces material, labor, and capital as the primary raw assets.

No doubt, there will always be some jobs where the emphasis is on all but mindless labor: flipping hamburgers; rote assembly line work that at least temporarily defies automation; or perhaps the most menial road construction work. But thankfully, most of us are going to be able to use our God-given, unique, and creative brains as we earn our daily bread as knowledge workers.

Where Have All the Secretaries Gone?

The information age based job transformation of the office secretary over the past thirty years is a common, but certainly dramatic example of the evolution of the knowledge worker. A secretarial job description in those former days was all encompassing; essentially handling anything the boss either could not or would not do for himself, starting with making a pot of fresh coffee each and every morning. But the litmus test for getting a secretarial job in that era was the ability to flawlessly spell, type, and punctuate sixty words per minute. A barrier that kept many an ambitious file clerk from occupying a desk just outside the corner office.

Today, because of the word processing revolution we do not find many secretaries at the office any more. More likely we will see a much smaller number of very highly qualified "executive assistants." These assistants help to put together the key presentations, evaluate the next generation of office suite software, set-up large international meetings, and make complex travel arrangements all via computer. Rather than spending hours combing through rows of drab gray filing cabinets for misplaced company documents, as in former times, they now search the Internet for obscure, but market-important information on future vehicle production in Thailand or current electric power usage in Brazil. We may not know how many words per minute these men and women, who now comprise this elite cadre of executive assistants can type, but we do know that it would be rather stupid, pointless, and insulting to ask!

"Six Months Ago I Couldn't Even Spell Auther And Now I Are One!"

So far we have discussed how the computer and the Internet allow people to work more productively, and at the same time greatly extend the boundaries of their former job descriptions. But there is a third, and often more-powerful aspect that is also operative: the computer/Internet is empowering many individuals to engage as agents of change in totally new and exciting lines of job endeavors. Busy homemakers can now become stock-market "day traders," while others can open lucrative cyberspace storefronts starting with nothing more than a well thought out idea and an eye-catching web page.

The greatly enhanced ability to write and publish is yet another example. All of us have a story to tell, and a dream of telling that story some day in the form of a best selling book. But we are also well aware of some seemingly big hurdles that have plagued us ever since the days we had to write a ten-sentence book report, back in grade school. Maybe we:

1. Can't read our own handwriting five minutes later.
2. Can't spell worth a darn.
3. Tend to toss words around like small boats on a raging sea, or bulldoze whole paragraphs.
4. Turn a simple thought into a sentence that runs on for miles.
5. Two-finger type that makes words like "the" and "that" come out "teh" and "taht."
6. Can't figure out when to use a colon, a semi-colon, or a period.
7. Never get to write for more than an hour or two at a time, and then only in the middle seat of a cramped airplane.
8. Hate to create a starting outline, even for a book that is a couple hundred pages long.

Well, if you find yourself "challenged" by any, or all of the above, do not be discouraged. Just have at it with your great new novel "For Whom the Buzzer Rings." Be assured that these mostly mechanistic hurdles can be overcome with a modest laptop computer, and what is now pretty routine word processing software. Ordinary software that does among other things, file management, revision control, checks spelling and punctuation, and makes outlining simple. This is not to say that the computer doesn't come with its own unique set of headaches. For example, an entire chapter might go into long-term hiding by accidentally pressing the wrong "Control-Alt" key combination. And it seems that the laptop battery invariably gives out during those rare and inspired moments of literary genius. But overall the word processor has proved to be an extraordinary enabler for the modern writer.

The Computer/Internet Alters Traditional Power Balances.

It is hard to forecast all the ways that this computer-supercharged concept of knowledge management will change our daily working styles. It is speculated, for example, that a majority of employees will no longer need to journey to a common workplace each day, rather they will be able to work at home. Even today, sitting close to the boss no longer defines the office elite; rather the "in crowd" are those directly and continuously linked to his PC—possibly thousands of miles away!

One trend is already clear: The still juvenile Internet is already altering traditional power relationships based on information access. Information on the Internet is for all practical purposes available to all comers. And only to a slightly lesser extent is the specialized software used to manipulate and evaluate this data. This general availability of data radically alters the competitive advantage between two or more suppliers of the same product or service. In the past companies accumulated knowledge of markets, processing techniques, and suppliers rather slowly. This information was often gathered at great expense, and was, therefore, carefully guarded. Now, the computer/Internet makes much of this same kind of information available to a potential start-up competitor in a matter of hours.

Even more significantly, because of e-commerce, traditional customers often are being transformed into empowered competitors. Stockbrokers, auto dealers, real estate agents and many other types of traditional middlemen have already experienced this trend.

Summary.

The computer and Internet impact the manner in which we work in several important ways:

1. This combination allows us to gather data far more quickly and far more thoroughly than in former times. Our evaluation capabilities are thus greatly enhanced. So too, are our abilities to create beneficial change in a timely fashion. These capabilities in turn alter the external market leverage between customers and providers.
2. The computer/Internet gives further impetus to a much broader class of knowledge workers. It expands the dimensions and expectations of our traditional job functions. And it empowers individuals to pursue entirely new fields of useful endeavors.

3. Complexity, cyclicality, and variability characterize knowledge work. Because of these three factors knowledge work demands a high degree of collaboration, and a management style of remote trust and risk tolerance.

Discussion Problems.

1. Based on your current computer literacy give five examples that illustrate how the computer and Internet either enhances your job-effectiveness, or puts you at a relative disadvantage to others.

2. List five job functions in your organization, which require heavy knowledge management skills.

3. List five job functions, with which you are personally familiar, that have either been eliminated or the need for personnel greatly reduced because of "computerization."

4. Using the Internet, find a list of the fifty fastest growing companies in the US. What percentage of these companies have products or services that are primarily in the area of Knowledge Management?

5. Define the nature of the personal "value-added" to your work products.

6. For each of the following jobs identify those areas where the process of knowledge work comes into play:
   a) Professional baseball player.
   b) "Stand-up" comedian.
   c) Automotive mechanic.
   d) Prison guard.

Chapter 9—The Seven Levers Of Enterprise Change

Throughout most of the previous pages we have concentrated on the attitude and approach that make for a job-effective change agent. In this chapter we want to address a related question: "What are the key ways by which the agent of change actually brings about meaningful change in an enterprise?" An answer to this important question can be found by considering seven powerful operating levers that are common to every successful business. An understanding of the role that each of these levers plays in moving a business forward will provide us with valuable guidance in our own individual efforts to effect beneficial change.

A Look At "The System."

Every successful business operates around a system. Simply put, the system controls the way the work happens to get done in a particular enterprise. In this sense the working system of an enterprise is very much like the operating system of a computer. To use the computer effectively we need to have a good understanding of the operating system. Unlike computers, however, that tend to use just one of a few available operating systems, say Windows ®, the operating system of a particular enterprise tends to be highly specific as a result of its:

1. Organizational reporting structures.
2. Past experiences, traditions, and cultural values of the workforce.

3. Products and services.
4. Downstream customers.
5. Upstream suppliers.

One cannot, therefore, read a book on the way business takes place at General Motors and validly conclude that the same system operates at Cisco, or Procter & Gamble. Indeed, a book on GM will prove to be of only a little help in understanding Ford Motor Company. So as a starting point, a job-effective change agent must be willing to invest the time to learn first-hand the working system of the specific organization in which he or she is employed. Agents of change must also see this as a continual learning process, because every organization's system has a highly evolving character in today's fast-changing world of enterprise. For example: a new CEO sets a new direction; the biggest competitor is suddenly from the Far East; laser technology revamps a fundamental manufacturing process; or employees switch to "flex time." All of which impact the system to one degree or another.

While enterprise operating systems may be unique to, and dynamic within a specific organization, our approach to learning about a given system can be common. This is because every successful enterprise is guided by a clear *mission,* and employs a set of common resources to accomplish that mission. These universally employed resources are:

1. Markets.
2. Materials.
3. Money.
4. Machines.
5. Management.
6. Manpower.

Every business needs customers; uses materials and machines to create products and services; must have money to pay its employees and suppliers; and lastly, must have the manpower and a guiding management to effectively carry out its mission. It is easy to remember this set of six resources, along with the guiding mission, as the "7-M's" of enterprise. However, it is more important to understand that they are the seven operating levers by which a change agent moves a business forward.

Most of us enjoy playing "sidewalk superintendent," as a large building is being constructed. The operator of the gigantic derrick crane always captures our immediate attention. Seated behind a bank of control levers, he uses one set to swing the crane left or right, another set to move the boom up or down, a third pair to extend or retract that boom, and still another group to open or close the bucket. We marvel at the smooth, yet powerful and complex crane movements radiating from his highly practiced hands. We might even like to be in the operator's cab ourselves!

Seeing ourselves with opportunities to control the progress of enterprise is a fitting image for today's change agent. All of us can effect great change in the building and re-building of an enterprise by skillfully operating the powerful levers of mission, markets, materials, money, machines, management, and manpower.

For example, if an executive wishes to change the culture of the organization so that it brings new products to market much more rapidly than in the past, he or she will do so by adroitly manipulating one or more of these levers. Perhaps, the executive will streamline the management structure so that decisions can be made more quickly, and at the same time expand the R&D manpower. Similarly, a marketing manager intent on expanding sales might decide to spend more money on advertising, extend the geographical reach of the company's markets, and change the compensation plan for the sales force. Lastly, engineers often fulfill their responsibilities as contributors to customer-valued change by employing new materials in their designs, or new machines to more efficiently fabricate their products.

Mission Determines All.

The first and most important of the seven M's is mission. Every serious enterprise activity we pursue has a carefully thought-out objective called the mission. This objective may range from building a nuclear-powered aircraft carrier, providing quarterly financial reports, or overhauling tired engines. The mission is a very special kind of objective because it has the basic connotation of providing a valuable service or useful product *to others*. For this reason church groups and military organizations speak often about their particular mission. Inherent in the notion of mission are a strong sense of dedication and a clarity of purpose on the part of those called to carry it out. These two elements, when fully developed, become powerful success factors in the achievement of the end objective.

In a commercial enterprise, mission provides a like role. It is an organization's driving vision of the needs of its customers, patients, or clients, whatever the case may be.
Mc Donald's, for example, has described their mission in these words:

"Mc Donald's vision is to be the world's best quick service restaurant experience."

They further amplify the expression of this missionary vision as follows:

"Mc Donald's created the quick-service restaurant industry, and we are committed to maintaining our

leadership role, through close attention to quality, service, cleanliness, and value." [21]

These statements give unmistakable guidance—a kind of golden rule—to all Mc Donald's employees from the Oakbrook, Illinois corporate offices to a start-up kitchen in China. It tells them how their customers are always to be served. Moreover, it is a lasting guidance where the *what* of the mission, the "best quick service restaurant experience," does not change from year to year or vary among the 115 countries worldwide, where Mc Donald's has establishments.

This is an important characteristic of a properly adopted mission; its *essence* does not ordinarily change or suffer from "mission creep." Mc Donald's would soon no longer be Mc Donald's if it began to substitute Chateau Briand and Beef Wellington for Big Mac's and Chicken Nuggets. Or if it took down the golden arches and went to a candlelight ambiance in an attempt to attract the gourmet dining set.

On the other hand, the *how* of a mission can, and often must change. There are always better ways to speed-up service, improve quality, increase value, or pay stricter attention to cleanliness. For example, in the late nineties Mc Donald's adopted a "Made for You" cooking scheme, and added breakfast bagels and soups to the menu, in an effort to meet shifting customer tastes and a growing older population. Similarly, Mc Donald's offers mutton burgers in the sacred-cow country of India. So the *how* of the mission provides perpetually fertile fields for the agents of change.

That Mc Donald's has grown from a mid-fifties hamburger "joint" to a worldwide corporation today with annual sales of $40 billion dollars is a magnificent example of maintaining the *what* of the mission while continually improving the *how*.

It is always a challenge for an enterprise to continually adapt the *how* of their mission while remaining true to a still valid *what.* AT&T, for example, has struggled, since the mid-nineties, with the best way to redefine the *how* of their hundred year-old communications mission. In AT&T's words they must, "change from a long distance company to an 'any distance' company; from being a domestic to a global enterprise; from narrowband technology to broadband; and from fixed circuits to wireless."[22]

Goals Are Not The Mission.

An enterprise has other internal objectives that differ from the mission, which are called goals. Making a healthy profit is an essential goal if a business is going to grow. And wanting to be number one in a particular market is certainly a worthy goal. But both must be in harmony with the primary mission if the enterprise is going to prosper over the long haul. George W. Merck expressed it this way in 1950:

"We try never to forget that medicine is for the people. It is not for the profits. The profits follow, and if we have remembered that, they have never failed to appear. The better we have remembered that, the larger they have been." [23]

The benefits of that philosophy to Merck, its customer-patients, and shareholders over the last fifty years are one of the great stories of enterprise.

Unfortunately, the danger is always real that internal goals, however desirable, replace the mission, however important. It is a danger, which the job-effective agent of change must always be aware.

To summarize, job-effective agents of change continually look for ways to improve the *how* of an established and validated mission within the framework of the *what*. He or she will always be sure that internal goals are not to the detriment of the external mission.

The Six Supporting M's.

Common to achieving all enterprising missions is the supportive presence of the remaining six-M's: markets, materials, money, machines, management, and manpower. These resource elements provide change agents at every level inexhaustible opportunities to improve the *how* or overall effectiveness of the mission.

Of course, the relative needs for each of these subordinate elements will vary widely depending on the business objective. Producing and selling automobiles will continually demand astronomic quantities of all six factors, while the requirements may be intermittent and minimal for a "mom and pop" sandwich shop. The essential point here is that a business enterprise grows in size and survives profitably only when the relative usage of the six- M's have been carefully optimized, based on the missionary objective to be achieved. In other words, employed in such a way that makes sense on a total systems basis.

So, we would not use expensive manpower to do what a simple machine can do better and quicker. We employ light, tough, and expensive titanium for airplane wing structures, but certainly not for "2x4" studs in home construction. Lastly, we would not waste our money advertising women's dress shoes in a hunting and fishing magazine, no matter how widely circulated. These examples point out a corollary proposition: every failure of an enterprise with a valid mission is sooner or later traceable to either the lack or misuse of one or more of these six supporting resources.

The Change Power of The Six Resource Levers.

Needless to say, there are countless ways by which we might go about effecting change in an enterprise with a well-defined mission. But the leverage power of markets, materials, money, machines, management, and manpower stand out for two vital reasons:

1. These resource elements have a synergistic impact on each other and sometimes even on themselves, well beyond what we might first expect. For example, a new, tougher steel material makes a new machine possible. That same new machine easily stamps components from a previously unworkable material. Or, one man designs a machine that ends up freeing ten other men to do something more productive. Money in the form of profits often has this multiplying effect; when wisely reinvested, it reaps still more profits. Lastly, an established market becomes the launching pad for entirely new markets. The advent of computers created the market opportunities for a dozen different peripherals. The appearance of a PC on nearly every desk also made the Internet a fantastic reality; and the Internet, in turn, makes possible "e-commerce" in its endless variations. This re-enforcement effect provides the momentum that allows a healthy business not only to sustain itself, but greatly expand as well.

2. Each of these supporting resources serves as an enterprise channel through which flow the major economic, technological, and social forces of a given era. Hence, because of current economic forces, we must now view our marketplace to be Southeast Asia just as much as the southeastern United States. As a result of the advances in technology, we must continually update our machines if we are to provide our goods and services competitively. And because of changing demographics our manpower pools must fully embrace those workers who happen to be somehow different than ourselves.

We will next examine just a few of the many key roles that each of the six supporting levers of change can play in moving an enterprise forward. And we want to develop some sense of the direction each resource lever is currently trending. By becoming more acquainted with the nature of these transformations, the change agent is better prepared to make use of these system levers in the future.

We will also see that the last three of these resource levers — machines, management, and manpower— affect each of us in a very personal and sometimes threatening sort of way: a new machine might surpass us in a hard-won skill area; a long used management style may no longer be appropriate; and a job position, we really value, may terminate abruptly. Machines, management, and manpower present agents of change with the most difficult challenge of all—the foresight and willingness to continually change themselves.

****

Markets.

The market is the acid test of our business mission. However finely we craft our products, or tailor our offered services, if there are no customers, who either want or can afford to buy them, we have failed! The market of the twenty-first century is a "good news-bad news" story: markets are truly global in their reach. Customers are now everywhere, but on the down side, so too, are the competitors. These customers are all knowing; they know what products and services the competition has to offer, and for how much. The consumer knows precisely what he or she wants today. But it is a transient knowing! Tomorrow it is liable to be something very different. So, customers tend to be very fickle! To illustrate the point, how much are we willing to pay today for a PC that we thought was the latest and greatest six months ago? Because of these market-related changes, we are in the midst of a rapid transition from an age of mass production to the era of "mass customization."

Customers Are Starting To Look A Lot Different Than Before!

The demographics of the marketplace are also rapidly changing. First of all, we as a nation are growing older simply because that dominant cohort known as the "baby boomers" are now into their fifties. Just as significantly, we are each living longer. Overall life expectancy in the year 2000 is 76.4 years; up from 70.8 years in 1970. This is a gain that averages out to two months per year thanks to advances in medical care, and the adoption of healthier life styles over that thirty-year period. It is a nice dividend we are receiving for just happening to be alive during this time period!

The combined effects of the aging of the "baby boomer" generation and improved longevity will send the US senior population, 65 and older, soaring. It will nearly double from the present 32 million to 62 million by 2025. This aging trend is true of most of the Western world. Accompanying this increasing age pattern will be the correspondingly changed needs for products and services in the marketplace: more blood pressure pills than birth control pills; and as many senior citizen centers as kindergartens.

We are also becoming more of a "rainbow" society as African Americans, Hispanics, and Asians increasingly become larger fractions of the total society. Again, as the cultural and economic influences of these diverse groups expand, we can expect corresponding opportunities and displacements in the marketplace. In the successful companies of the future, a broad-based network of change agents will have translated these demographic changes into expanding opportunities long before they become threatening displacements.

They Don't Always Shop Where They Used To Either!

As much as market demographics have seen profound shifts in the last twenty years, agents of change have been busy devising new delivery systems to tap those markets. Just consider the competition that now confronts Sears, Penny's, Macy's, and Marshall Field's—each venerable and secure members of a virtual merchant oligarchy just a generation ago. Among the bigger new kids on the block are:

1. Wal Mart
2. Best Buy
3. Home Depot
4. Toys 'R Us
5. Home Shopping Network
6. Amazon.com
7. E-Bay.

Each newcomer was brought into being by change agents that saw how a different delivery system to the end customer could be translated into massive competitive advantage. This is an excellent example of how change agents can effectively exploit the market through new business models of enterprise.

****

Materials.

The New Age Of Molecules.

For most of the twentieth century we lived simultaneously in three material ages—the Oil Age, the Steel Age, and the Atomic age. A nation's economic power and world standing became inextricably linked to barrels of oils held in reserve, tons of steel produced, and kilograms of uranium refined. But the later years of the twentieth century gave birth to still another new material age. What we might call the Molecular Age. We have learned to polymerize oil into countless engineered plastics, and to process tiny slivers of silicon into powerful microprocessors. We have discovered how to combine complex organic compounds into milligram doses of life-saving antibiotics, and how to carry ten thousand voice and data signals simultaneously over a hair-sized optical fiber. The promise of this Molecular Age becomes even more astounding as we begin to explore gene engineering and "nano-mechanics."

Silicon chips, and pharmaceutical pills dramatize the key points of the fundamental changes inherent in our modern exploitation of materials. Their value is no longer to be measured in metric tons produced or barrels shipped. Rather, the value of these new materials is to be measured in the accumulated scientific knowledge of the subtle molecular transformations that make these new materials possible.

So it is not so much a nation's native mineral resources that now matter; it is changing rapidly to its intellectual resources. New riches are more likely to be discovered under the microscope than with drilling rigs! Laboratory petri dishes are becoming the new blast furnaces of productivity.

Correspondingly, the change agents are not those captains of industry such as John D. Rockefeller and Andrew Carnegie, who marshaled enormous resources and built vast, process plants. Instead they are the new breeds of semiconductor physicists, chemists and genetic engineers that exploit quantum phenomena, create molecular transformations and manipulate DNA on the very fringes of life itself. A half-century ago Winston Churchill wisely predicted, "The empires of the future are the empires of the mind." Our minds have now become the storehouses of our enterprise treasures.

We have come to understand that all of recorded history has been just a prolonged infancy in the realm of effective material usage. The secrets of real exploitation have eluded us, until recently, only a little less than the alchemists of the Middle Ages. But now armed with our rapidly growing knowledge of the molecular science of materials, we stand ready to journey along a very broad road of new and revolutionary changes. It is a fantastic world of opportunities that is being brought about by the new agents of material change.

****

Money.

Two little kids setting up a sidewalk lemonade stand on a hot summer day illustrate well the fundamental leveraging effect of money in an enterprise; it takes money to make money! In fact, it is regularly reported that the single biggest reason for the failure of a start-up business is insufficient capital. One boy's dad has to finance the purchase of paper cups and lemons, even if the other boy's mom supplies the sugar, napkins, and ice gratis.

And so a business needs it's shareholders and lenders to get it started, keep it moving forward, and bear the considerable risks along the way. We might think of this function of money as the oil that lubricates the entire enterprise engine; from purchase of first raw stocks and equipment at the input end, on through the back end payment of the workers wages and dividends to the stockholders.

The New Way Of Counting Profits.

But there is another new money lesson revealed at this little lemonade stand that has special relevance to our change-accelerating world of business and commerce. It is the concept of profits as a *residual,* which is increasingly displacing the textbook "mark-up-over-cost" approach to profit determination. By residual, we simply mean that which is leftover after all expenses are paid.

More than likely our little friends will not price their refreshments based on their costs plus a fair return of say twenty-five percent. Rather, after a little market sleuthing, they will set their price to exactly match what the kids in the next block, their competition, are charging per cup. So, at the end of that first hot afternoon, as they count up their receipts, and painfully recall that they still owe Dad $2.12 for materials, they will be left with a single hope—a hope that they sold enough eight-cent servings of lemonade to still be able to treat themselves to a couple of ice cream cones.

Precisely the same situation takes place today in the general business world. As a consequence of global competition and omniscient consumerism, there is an inescapable market dynamic that governs the acceptable price for virtually every product independently of an individual supplier's costs. Thus, stringent control of product or service costs becomes the only possible way a company can hope to make a profit. It is a fact of enterprise life about which today's job-effective change agent must be ever mindful.

This new reality of profits as a residual has been made unmistakably clear by the many painful changes taking place in American businesses starting in the mid-eighties. Corporations, long-accustomed to passing-along costs under a broad inflation umbrella, now paid quickly and dearly for those earlier, heady days with downsizings, and wage and fringe benefit reductions in order to just survive.

Notwithstanding the resultant and widespread discontent, there is a little reason to believe that these competition-induced changes will slow down in the coming years, much less end. On the bright side, as some companies still struggle with these issues, savvy change agents in others have turned these same issues into profitable advantage by re-engineering their business in a way that is unencumbered by the lax and bloated practices of the past.

****

Machines

In a fundamental way the evolution of machines is synonymous with the progress of enterprise. This history is all about agents of change finding new and ingenious ways to accomplish work that was beyond either the physical strengths or mental inclinations of both men and beasts. The full blossoming of this pursuit brought forth the Industrial Revolution, beginning with James Watt's steam engine. Starting with this development, we can distinguish six types of machines that have had profound influence on the modern world of enterprise; each development often building on the one before it, and enabling enterprises to expand in a new direction, or reach a still more productive plateau. These seminal machines[24] are, in the rough order in which they made their first appearances:

1. Load moving heat engines.
2. Electrical transforming machines.
3. Communication machines.
4. Mechanical repeating machines.
5. Self-adapting machines.
6. Information processing machines.

Table 9.1 summarizes the key technologies underlying each of these machine developments and highlights the major benefits each successively brought to enterprise. For example, because of machine progress America's agricultural needs, along with a generous share of food exports, are handled today by less than four percent of the workforce. This is a ten-fold reduction since 1900. Similarly, despite a continually growing abundance and variety of products, improvements in machine productivity have allowed the manufacturing sector of the labor force to trend downward from about thirty percent in 1960 to about twenty percent in 2000.[25]

Since the Industrial Revolution machine capabilities have rapidly expanded in four dimensions: they have become physically more powerful, faster, much more precise, and increasingly "smarter." One can only wonder how tomorrow's agents of change will continue this expansion with such new technologies as fusion, the laser, fuel cells, and broadband wireless communication. Surely, there will be countless innovative new products, along with today's already familiar ones that will be made quicker, better, and cheaper.

But this same four-fold expansion of machinery has also had a profound and continuing impact on us as individual workers—sometimes good, at other times bad. Mechanical and electric power remove all practical physical limits as to what we might build or make; modern communication systems eliminate the geographic boundaries as to where, with whom, and at what hours we may work; and information processing machines have become the engines driving the "New Economy"

On the other hand, load moving machines have swept away the pick-and-shovel laborer; repeating machines have often chained the factory worker to the assembly line; automation continually threatens the unskilled; and most recently the computer and the Internet divides us digitally. Perhaps more than any other enterprise factor, it is machines that permanently sort each of us out as "changers" or "changees."

Approx. First Use	Machine Type	Example Technologies	Benefits To Enterprise	Impact On Workers
1720	Combustion Engines	Steam, Gasoline, Diesel	Tireless physical power to move loads.	Pollution, safety issues, devaluing of manual labor.
1850	Electric transforming machines	Transformers, motors & generators	Controllable power to do work remotely	Pollution, safety issues, further devaluing of manual labor.
1870	Communication machines	Telegraph, telephone, radio, fax, cell phone	Ability of an enterprise to respond greatly enhanced.	Generally not significant.
1870	Repeating machines	Mechanically- driven boring, punching, and stamping machines	Mass production emerges.	Assembly line mentality takes root.
1940	Self-adapting machines	Electronically controlled assembly and processing machines	Automation, "zero-defects" quality, and mass customization become realities.	Need for unskilled blue collar workers begins to diminish.
1950	Information processing machines.	Software- programmed digital processors. Internet.	New Economy arises based on information and services.	Digital divide begins to separate the white collar workforce.

Table 9.1. Impact of Key Machines On Enterprise Since The Industrial Revolution. (page 187)

****

Management

It was powered machinery that gave birth to the Industrial Revolution, but it was the Industrial Revolution that, in turn, fathered a widespread management philosophy, which became known as "Scientific Management." This philosophy offered a powerful operational approach, but, which we will see, frequently works at cross-purposes to the needs of today's fast-paced and ever-changing world of enterprise.

Following the Civil War the railroads began to crisscross the nation, and small owner-operated fabrication shops rapidly grew into large factory businesses, as the pace of the Industrial Revolution quickened. Prior to that time little consideration was given to the qualifications and formal training of the workforce. Instead workers were hired on a trial basis, and performed their tasks as best they knew how, but always under the watchful eyes of the owner–operators.

The spreading reaches of railroad tracks no longer permitted close worker supervision. Yet, there could be a dangerous safety issue if an engineer decided on his own to reschedule the departure of his distant train by even a few minutes. The advent of large factories created similar kinds of problems. Keeping a close eye on the individual productivity of three or four hundred untrained employees was a practical impossibility, even though they might be located within the same building complex. Nor would it do for an expensive piece of processing machinery, such as a blast furnace, to be erratically fed with raw materials, depending on the uneven productivity of those workers charged with the loading of coke and iron ore. Lastly, a third related issue came along with the rise of large industrial organizations: with their need for huge capital, the single working owner became increasingly displaced by groups of passive investors with little understanding of the day to day operations of the enterprise. So there arose a companion need to hire professional managers to "run" the business.

The Answer Of Scientific Management.

These three growing managerial problems created interest in ideas and theories on improving the efficiency of large operations. Foremost among the proponents of Scientific Management was Frederick Taylor, a lawyer who later became a mechanical engineer. Taylor was a prolific "hands-on" type of engineer, who was awarded over 100 patents. But his enduring contributions were in laying the foundations for modern industrial management practice.

Taylor's root idea was to create a clear dichotomy of responsibilities to achieve a given work task: there would be a management group and a laboring group. A clear divide between brains and muscles! The managers would plan down to the last detail what had to be done, and organize and train each member of the work force to do a repetitive aspect of a job task. Finally the managers would control and evaluate the work as it progressed.

Others, following in Taylor's footsteps, refined the concepts of planning, controlling, and organizing into a management dogma that was the enterprise equivalent of the theological trinity. Implicit in these concepts of planning, controlling and organizing were:

1. Exactly what must be done to successfully complete a job task can clearly be *established beforehand*.
2. There is a best, standardized way of doing a job that can be determined by a series of *scientifically controlled experiments.*

3. The *management always knows better* than the workers the proper way of doing a job.

Scientific Management drew a large following, and over time was adopted by a wide range of industries. Where work efforts could be broken down by the managers into highly repetitive sub-tasks, these concepts worked rather well, especially on the complex, high volume manufacturing assembly lines, and in the material processing industries. In principle, one could apply the same basic concepts with equal ease to the assembly of automobiles, the making of ready-to-wear dresses, or the processing of chickens.

However, in practice the necessary managerial knowledge to effectively plan, control, and organize was often highly specific to a particular industry, and learned only slowly over time. This gave strong and lasting impetus to the notion that the most knowledgeable managers were always the most senior ones. Those who, in effect, possessed the fullness of the company's tribal knowledge by having long "been there and done that."

This tribal knowledge, narrowly held, covered broad expanses. Not only did it encompass the best way to set-up a plant to manufacture a company's widgets, but also included the knowledge of such unspoken things as which customer would be most tolerant of a shipping delay; which product lines were the "stars," and which were the "dogs"; and how competitors were likely to react if the selling price of widgets were raised another ten percent.

Service Work and Scientific Management Do Not Always Mix Well!

In our higher helicopter view of the economy, we noted that we have rapidly become a service economy, which employs roughly three out of four American workers today. This compares with twenty percent around 1900, when

Scientific Management came into vogue. Now, in contrast with typical manufacturing assembly line work of, say, putting the same nut on the same bolt so many times per minute, service work often requires a high degree of flexibility to changing circumstances. Thus, there is a far narrower applicability to Taylor's principles. Moreover, the quality aspect of the service work is often far more important than the quantity aspect, in the determination of a successful outcome.

It is true that planning, controlling, and organizing may work very well in developing a routine for the "assembling" of Big Macs at service-oriented Mc Donald's. But what about setting standards for a group of engineers writing software code at IBM? A software development manager cannot judge the progress of the work simply by tracking the number of lines of code written per day by his team. As we know only too well from "Y2K," software mistakes can be very costly. Like termites that set up housekeeping in the foundation beams of a building, the destructiveness of software "bugs" is often discovered only after the near collapse of the entire program structure. So the manager must constantly balance his getting-the-job-done expectations with sometimes unpredictable and time-consuming efforts that must be expended in the careful documentation and checking of the code.

Of course, standards and procedures may be written for any kind of service work. Rules may be set for when a policeman draws his gun; there are documented procedures for landing an airplane; and there are even established protocols for neurological surgery. But the on-the-spot judgment of the policeman, pilot, or surgeon in the application of these rules supremely determines the outcome. Similarly, performing a computerized "what-if" analysis of a pending business purchase; tailoring a life insurance policy to a client's particular needs; or even selling a pair of shoes to a fussy customer, all require a great deal of spontaneous judgment on the part of the person actually doing the work.

In other forms of service work the prescribed tribal operating rules don't work very well at all. What good is an elaborate and long-established procedure for making a hamburger in India? How do you go about getting three competitive bids for a plant construction in the state-controlled economy of China? How useful are a company's age-old, rigid pricing formulas against competitors that have highly job-specific, computerized quoting processes? Here we see examples where real-time, adaptive learning becomes more important than long term tribal experience.

Lessons Learned On the Telephone.

All of us have had the frustrating experience of trying to "star-star-pound" our way through an automated telephone-answering menu. How we wish for the days when there was a real live person at the other end who could quickly rout a call into the deepest reaches of a cavernous organization. It is a sorry example of how a service that has been totally *planned, controlled, and organized,* miserably limps along in practice. Similarly, it takes us only a few seconds after answering a telephone to sense that a mono-toned tele-marketer is mechanically reading a planned, controlled, and organized script. Our only thought is how to end the intrusion quickly and firmly. More often than not, rigid planning, controlling and organizing prove to be clumsy and blunt managerial tools when it comes to service work!

Scientific Management And the Information Age Do Not Always Mix Well Either.

The arrival of the Information Age has also dealt Scientific Management a further setback. The power implications of key business information is no longer the same. With the rise of the knowledge worker, the information-is-power balance has tilted more and more in the direction of those who have the ability to perform a comprehensive "what-if" computer analysis of a complex financial deal, and to those who can quickly search the Internet to obtain some obscure, but decision-crucial statistic. Suffice to say here that the traditional, one-sided decision making authority of managers has been further blurred by the growing importance of these individuals in the success of an enterprise. The related question immediately arises, "How does one now effectively control a group of workers, who operate most of their working day in the far reaches of cyberspace?"

In many traditional hierarchical organizations the exercise of power has, in fact, been frequently effected through the retention of information and its highly selective dispersal by the management. Today, however, the computer savvy individual can in short order become expert in market demographics for a product, or can quickly software model the estimated profitability of a proposed service. Fully armed with the facts, and buttressed by a raft of computerized analyses, he or she may become far more inclined to challenge the boss on a decision where a plant should be located, or how many widgets to produce for the Christmas season. The managerial mantra of "We have always done it this way" no longer ends all discussions! Once again we see the impact of the digital divide brought about by the information age.

Looked at from the positive side, a properly motivated, broadly information-empowered organization is a formidable competitive advantage for a manager. Jack Welch of GE, puts it this way, "An organization's ability to learn, and translate that learning into action rapidly, is the ultimate competitive business advantage."[26]

Emperors Without Clothes.

Three trends have converged within a generation to undermine the role of the traditional "scientific" manager:

1. The greatly accelerated pace of decision making required by global competition and the strong advantage of "time-to-market."

2. The need for flexible, on-the-spot decision making inherent in a service oriented economy.

3. The broad diffusion of enterprise-vital knowledge brought on by the Information Age.

Each of these trends has collectively worn thin the planning, controlling, and organizing clothing of traditional management practice. These garments were woven together with two rather tenuous threads: First, that changes in the ongoing business environment would continue to be slow, or at very least, highly predictable. Second, that it was quite possible to separate the "thinking" and the "doing" responsibilities of a business. Clearly, these premises are no longer the case.

Today's manager needs to put on a new kind of garb if he or she wishes to be a job-effective agent of change. It is the garb of the *leader*. To repeat an earlier expressed, but crucial idea, a leader provides his working team more with tomorrow's vision than today's direction; and more with a compass setting than a detailed road map. The managerial leader empowers his team with a remote trust far more than he directly controls, and he learns from his team as much as he teaches. Finally, today's leader plays in the game as much as he coaches from the sidelines.

****

Manpower.

The last of the 7- M's we want to explore for change is manpower. We have already detailed some of the impact that machines have had on working people throughout industrial history. And in the management section we have seen the need for role convergence that must take place between management and workers. We now come to the point of exploring some of the basic sociological changes taking place in the workplace today. We will see clear evidence of an increasingly diverse, and an increasingly smarter workforce. Both of which can provide the managerial agent of change with increased leverage to move the enterprise forward. But at the same time he or she will recognize some of the challenges brought about by an increasingly transient workforce.

The Workforce Is Changing Demographically.

Previously, it was noted that we are rapidly becoming an aging population, and much more racially and ethnically diverse. These trends of themselves will of necessity bring about profound changes in the workplace. Only a very few of us will be rich enough to start counting the golden years at age sixty. Also, it is no longer your father's kind of company! Today, women comprise 45% of the total workforce, compared to 31% in 1960. More than 40 % of these women have at least one child under seventeen.[27] The workplace change implications of this go far beyond sexual harassment issues. They involve matters of equal pay, competition, flex time, and our traditional notions of male and female roles at the office, and responsibilities at home.

Today's Workers Are Smarter And Working Harder.

We are increasingly becoming a better-educated work force. In 1970, fifty-two percent of all Americans completed high school. At that time only fourteen percent of the men and eight percent of the women had completed four or more years of college. By 1998 all these figures improved substantially: eighty-three percent of the population had completed high school; and twenty-seven percent of the men and twenty-two percent of the women had completed four or more years of college[28]. The net result being that we now have many more, (but still not enough!) workers who are better prepared as they enter the labor force.

The statisticians also tell us that on the average we are working significantly longer—47 hours per week versus 43 hours a decade ago.[29] At the same time they also tell us that we are becoming much more productive.[30] Today, each of us produces 20 percent more goods and services than we did in 1980. But that Friday night exhausted feeling tells us this same "harder and smarter" story in a wearisome, but so much more gripping sort of way.

Maybe Diamonds Are Forever But Certainly Not Jobs!

Figure 9.1 is a revealing graph on job tenure statistics based on a 1998 government survey.[31] This graph indicates that only 73% of the total working population have been with their current employer for at least one year. Only 44% of this population have stayed at least five years, and just 25% of the workers were around to receive their ten-year service award! When the specific cohort of male's aged 45-54 is considered, just half have been with their current employer for a ten-year period. Based on this survey data, the *median* stay for all workers with a single employer is 3.6 years. This leads to the prediction that people entering the workforce today will change employers on the average seven to nine times throughout their working career.[32] No wonder portable pension schemes are such a hot topic!

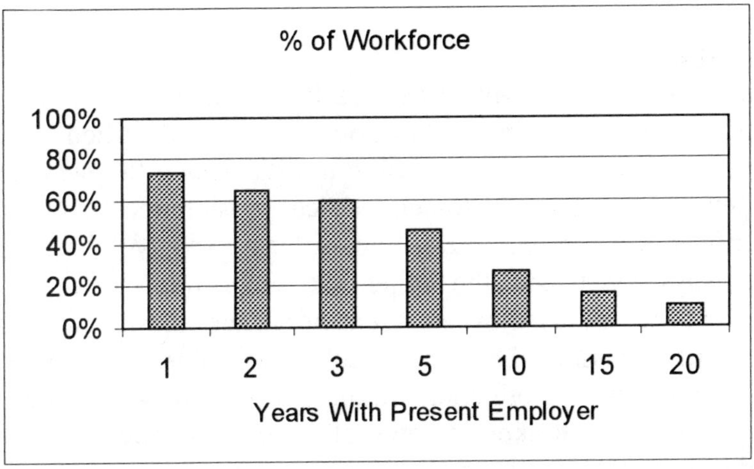

Figure 9.1. Long Employee Job Tenures Are Becoming Increasingly Rare.

Often younger employees with less than several year's tenure leave their jobs because either they see greener pastures elsewhere, or their employer determines that they are unsuited for a particular line of work. Statistics show 46% of the employees in the 25 to 34 age group change jobs in less than three years. More disturbing is the involuntary termination of job-effective workers, who have held their positions for three or more years. For example, during the full employment years of 1995-1997 over three and a half million workers in this category lost their jobs involuntarily. Plant shutdowns or plant relocations were reported to account for 47% of these losses. Another 21% were let go do to "slack work." Lastly, the remaining 32% were victims of position elimination.[33]

Unfortunately, it is apparent that even job-effective workers may find themselves casualties of enterprise change. Once again, a high degree of self-adaptability will serve an agent of change especially well during these times.

Summary.

The "Seven-M's,"—mission, markets, materials, money, machines, management, and manpower—were identified. We have seen the primacy of mission in establishing the *what* of an enterprise. This customer-focused mission must not be sacrificed for transient internal goals. Next, we have observed the ways by which the other six supporting "resource" elements can be used by the agent of change to influence the *how* of the mission. These powerful levers guide us along the clear pathways of effecting meaningful enterprise progress. Lastly, we have looked at some of the current ways that the major external forces of technology, economics, and social change express themselves through these resource elements, and alter the fortunes of an enterprise and its workers. It is the task of the change agent to maximize the opportunities presented, and to the greatest extent possible, diminish the threats.

Discussion Problems

1. In your own words, state your organization's mission statement.
2. What role can you personally play in changing the *what* and the *how* of your company's mission?
3. List three internal goals of your organization. Do they ever conflict with the mission?
4. How do markets, money, and materials impact the "system" in your organization?

5. What potential changes in machines, management, and manpower do you believe will impact you personally over the next three years? What will be the impact on your coworkers?

6. In your kind of business, where do you find people with many years of experience most valuable?

7. To what extent do the mangers in your organization function as *leaders*?

8. On a "one to five" scale, rank the relative importance of each of the seven levers of enterprise on your particular organization.

9. For your business, which of the seven levers are most effective in dealing with the major changes brought about by:
   a) Globalization.
   b) An economy increasingly dominated by services.
   c) The rapid proliferation of technology.

Some Final Thoughts

In the preceding pages, our purpose was to construct a useful road map to becoming an agent of change in the world of enterprise. In drawing that map we found that there were many stops along the way. First, we looked at the vastly increased need for change agents brought about by globalization, the move to a service oriented economy, and the proliferation of new technologies.

We then defined our overall job-effectiveness in terms of the personal attitudes, approach, and skill sets that we bring to a job task. We developed a three-step work process of gathering, evaluating, and implementing that helps us to systematically accomplish customer-desired beneficial change.

Next, we focused on the personal side of job-effectiveness by considering a vital sixpack of job attributes needed by today's change agent. We saw how the change agent continually and comfortably adapts himself or herself as either a team leader or a team player. And we considered what a change agent is *not* with a visit to the company zoo.

We studied how a change agent, guided by a personal strategic intent, continually increases that job-effectiveness by developing unique core competencies. And we observed how these skills come together in today's very important job role of knowledge worker.

Finally, we looked at seven very powerful levers to effect enterprise change—mission, markets, materials, money, machines, management, and manpower. We saw that there is a primacy of mission that establishes the *what* of an enterprise—the providing of a valuable product or service to others. The remaining six supportive resources, on the other hand, provide endless opportunities for the change agent to improve the *how* of that mission. They also provide us with a reckoning position of what we might expect in the way of not-too-distant enterprise change: nano-mechanic machines, molecular computers, gene therapy, a cashless society, a full-flowering of cyberspace commerce, virtual companies, and a wireless world. How exciting it is to see oneself as one of tomorrow's agent of change!

Throughout we have come to understand that being a job-effective agent of change is a continuing challenge; it is much more of an unending journey than a reached destination. Each day we must be prepared to set out anew on a sometimes weary journey of practice, practice, and practice. Occasionally recalling the following two thoughts on being an agent of change may fortify us along the way:

First, let us recall, what Henry Ford I liked to tell his sometimes hesitant associates, "If you believe that you can, or believe that you cannot, you will always be right." Nothing empowers an agent of change more than a sincerely held belief that "I can!" or as a team, "We can!" These words are the mantra key that opens up the greatest and only truly inexhaustible resource in our arsenal of change—*resourcefulness.*

Second, throughout this book we have frequently seen the interweaving of attitude and approach—the woof and warp of the cloth of job-effectiveness. A good attitude is entwined in the right task approach. There is an old saying about the way we perform our job, and the satisfaction value we receive in turn: "Some men see themselves simply as being about the task of laying bricks, while others perceive themselves as artisans creating a cathedral." Each day as we lay the brick walls of maximum job-effectiveness, we want to keep in mind that we are also trying to build the cathedral of job-satisfaction!

ENDNOTES

---

[1] See "Strategic Innovation In Established Companies," Constantinos Markides, Sloan Management review, Spring 1998

[2] Data source: "1998 International Financial Statistics Yearbook," published by the International monetary Fund

[3] Data source: "1999 Statistical Abstracts of the United States," Table #678

[4] Source: US Patent & Trademark Office.

[5] Derived From Standard & Poor's Index – December Averages.

[6] During the first half of the year 2000,This growth trend in the S&P index moderated despite very high rates of economic expansion and worker productivity. Most likely this index moderation was due to a series of six interest rate increases on the part of the Federal Reserve, and thus may prove to be a temporary pause.

[7] See, for example, "The Diversity of Life," Edward O. Wilson. W.W. Norton & Co. 1992.

[8] Quoted from "The Story of Civilization, Vol. 5, 'The Renaissance' pages 499-500, by Will Durant. Published by MJF Publications, New York, NY.

[9] See for example, "Mastering The Dynamics Of Innovation," James M. Utterback, 1994. Harvard Business School Press. Boston MA

[10] "The Seven Habits Of Highly Effective People," Stephen Covey,

[11] See for example, "Truman" by David Mc Cullough, Simon & Schuster, 1992.

[12] See, for example, "Developing Clinical Problem Skills," H. S. Barrows and G. C. Pickell, published by W. W. Norton & Co., 1991

[13] Quoted from USA Today, February 27th, 1997
[14] "The Hero With A Thousand Faces," Joseph Campbell. Princeton University Press.
[15] See for example, the defining articles on these two key concepts by C.K. Pralahad and Gary Hamel "Strategic Intent," Harvard Business Review, May-June 1989, and "The Core Competence Of The Corporation," Harvard Business Review May-June 1990.
[16] See for example "Do What You Do Best," W.J.Walsh, Technology Management, 3rd Edition. Published by Warren, Gorham & Lamont, 1994
[17] Reported in USA Today , 6/10/99
[18] "Developing Clinical Problem Skills," H.S.Barrows and G. C. Pickell, published by W.W. Norton & Co., 1991
[19] Reference: US Army CERL Report 95/32
[20] See for example, "The Intelligent Enterprise," J. B. Quinn, 1992.
[21] Quoted from 1998 Mc Donalds Annual Report
[22] Quoted from 1998 AT&T Annual Report
[23] Quoted from 1999 Merck Annual Report
[24] We are using "machine" here in the formal dictionary sense of "an apparatus consisting of interrelated parts with separate functions and used in the performance of some kind of work." Thus we include, "communication machines" and the Internet. See for example, "The Webster Encyclopedic Dictionary of the English Language"
[25] See "Intelligent Enterprise," James Bryan Quinn, The Free Press, 1992
[26] Quoted in Business Week, page 170, 6/28/98

[27] Derived from "1999 Statistical Abstracts of the United States," Table # 659
[28] Derived from "Statistical Abstract of The United States:1998" #261

[29] Reported by Newsweek , November 1999.
[30] Derived from "1999 Statistical Abstracts Of the United States": Data Tables #652 & #659.
[31] Figure based on "Distribution Of Workers By Tenure," 1999 Statistical Abstracts of the United States: data table #670
[32] Bureau of Labor Statistics Report, March 2000
[33] Derived from "1999 Statistical Abstracts of the United States," Table #672

INDEX